DISCOVERING
CAREERS FOR YOUR FUTURE

animals

Ferguson Publishing Company
Chicago, Illinois

Carol Yehling
Editor

Beth Adler, Herman Adler Design Group
Cover design

Carol Yehling
Interior design

Bonnie Needham
Proofreader

Library of Congress Cataloging-in-Publication Data

Discovering careers for your future. Animals.
        p. cm.
    ISBN 0-89434-360-2
1.Animal specialists—Vocational guidance—Juvenile literature. 2. Zoologists—Vocational guidance—Juvenile literature. [1. Animal specialists—Vocational guidance. 2. Zoology—Vocational guidance. 3. Vocational guidance.] I. Title: Animals. II. Ferguson Publishing Company.

SF80 .D57 2000
636'.0023—dc21

                                                                                00-037659

Published and distributed by
Ferguson Publishing Company
200 West Jackson Boulevard, Suite 700
Chicago, Illinois 60606
800-306-9941
www.fergpubco.com

Printed in the United States of America
X-9

Table of Contents

Introduction 1

Animal Breeders and Technicians 6

Animal Caretakers 10

Animal Shelter Workers 14

Animal Trainers 18

Aquarists 22

Biologists 26

Farmers 30

Horse Grooms 34

Marine Biologists 38

Naturalists 42

Park Rangers 46

Pet Groomers 50

Pet Sitters 54

Veterinarians 58

Veterinary Technicians 62

Wildlife Photographers 66

Zoo and Aquarium Curators 70

Zoo and Aquarium Directors 74

Zookeepers 78

Zoologists 82

Glossary 86

Index of Job Titles 90

Animals on the Web 92

Introduction

You may not have decided yet what you want to be in the future. And you don't have to decide right away. You do know that right now you are interested in animals. Do any of the statements below describe you? If so, you may want to begin thinking about what careers involve working with animals.

___Science is my favorite subject in school.

___I collect butterflies/insects.

___I am responsible for feeding and caring for our family pet.

___I enjoy visiting the zoo.

___I regularly watch television shows about animals and nature.

___I am concerned about endangered species.

___Horseback riding is my favorite hobby.

___I like to read stories about animals.

___I enjoy birdwatching.

___I often visit the aquarium.

___I belong to a 4H Club or Future Farmers of America.

___I like to adopt stray animals.

___My parents are farmers and I would like to continue the family business.

___I like to hike in the woods and watch for animals in the wild.

Discovering Careers for Your Future: Animals is a book about careers involving animals, from animal breeders and technicians to zoologists. People who work with animals help us better understand our environment. They study, care for, raise, train, and protect species, from amoebas to primates.

This book describes many possibilities for future careers with animals. Read through it and see how different animal careers are connected. For example, if you are interested in domestic animals, you will want to read the chapters on Animal Caretakers, Animal Shelter Workers, Farmers, Pet Groomers, Pet Sitters, and Veterinarians. If you are interested in wild animals, you will want to read the chapters on Biologists, Marine Biologists, Wildlife Photographers, Zookeepers, and Zoologists. Go ahead and explore!

What do they do?

The first section of each chapter begins with a heading such as "What Animals Trainers Do" or "What Veterinarians Do." It tells what it's like to work at this job. It describes typical responsibilities and assignments. You will find out about working conditions. Which animal workers work inside in offices or laboratories? Which ones work outside in all kinds of weather? What tools and equipment do they use? This section answers all these questions.

How do I prepare for a career involving animals?

The section called "Education and Training" tells you what schooling you need for employment in each job—a high school diploma, training at a junior college, a college degree, or more. It also talks about on-the-job training that you could expect to receive after you're hired, and whether or not you must complete an apprenticeship program.

How much do they earn?

The "Earnings" section gives the average salary figures for the job described in the chapter. These figures provide you with a general idea of how much money people with a particular job can make. Keep in mind that many people really earn more or less than the amounts given here because actual salaries depend on many different things, such as the size of the company; the location of the company; and the amount of education, training, and experience you have. Generally, but not always, bigger companies located in major cities pay more than smaller ones in smaller cities and towns, and people with more education, training, and experience earn more. Also remember that these figures are current averages. They will probably be different by the time you are ready to enter the workforce.

What will the future be like for careers involving animals?

The "Outlook" section discusses the employment outlook for each career: whether the total number of people employed in this career will increase or decrease in the coming years and whether jobs in this field will be easy or hard to find. These predictions are based on economic conditions, the size and makeup of the population, foreign competition, and new technology. Terms such as "faster than the average," "about as fast as the average," and "slower than the average," are terms used by the U.S. Department of Labor to describe job growth predicted by government data.

Keep in mind that these predictions are general statements. No one knows for sure what the future will be like. Also remember that the employment outlook is a general statement about an industry and does not necessarily apply to everyone. A determined and talented person may be able to find a job in an industry or career with the worst kind of outlook. And a person without ambition and the proper training will find it difficult to find a job even in a booming industry or career field.

Where can I find more information?

Each chapter includes a sidebar called "For More Info." It lists organizations that you can contact to find out more about the field and careers in the field. You will find names, addresses, phone numbers, and Web sites.

Extras

Every chapter has a few extras. There are photos that show workers in action. There are sidebars and notes on ways to explore the field, related jobs, fun facts, profiles of people in the field, or lists of Web sites and books that might be helpful. At the end of the book you will find a glossary and an index. The glossary gives brief definitions of words that relate to education, career training, or employment that you may be unfamiliar with. The index includes all the job titles mentioned in the book. It is followed by a list of animal-related Web sites.

It's not too soon to think about your future. We hope you discover several possible career choices. Happy hunting!

Animal Breeders and Technicians

What Animal Breeders and Technicians Do

Animal breeders and technicians help to breed, raise, and market a variety of farm animals. Other animal breeders work with domesticated animals kept as pets, such as song birds, parrots, and all dog and cat breeds. Even wildlife populations that are kept in reserves, ranches, zoos, or aquariums are bred with the guidance of a breeder or technician.

Breeders work to create better, stronger breeds of animals or to maintain good existing breeds. *Artificial-breeding technicians* collect and package semen for use in insemination. *Artificial insemination technicians* collect semen from the male species of an animal and artificially inseminate the female. Whether the breeding is done artificially or naturally, the goals are the same. *Cattle breeders* mate males and females to produce animals with desired traits such as leaner meat and less fat. *Horse and dog breed-*

US Department of Agriculture

An animal technician examines pigs that have been tested for common diseases that affect farm animals.

ers try to create more desirable animals. They want horses and dogs who perform well, move fast, and look beautiful.

For nonfarm animals, breeders usually work with several animals within a breed or species to produce offspring for sale. There are ranches that produce a large number of exotic animals, and some stables and kennels that run full-staff breeding operations, but most pet breeders work out of their homes.

Most breeders and technicians who work on farms specialize in one of two areas. Those who specialize in livestock production work with cattle, sheep, pigs, or horses. Those who specialize in poultry

EXPLORING

• Organizations such as 4-H Clubs (http://www. 4h-usa.org) and the national Future Farmers of America (http://www. ffa.org) offer good opportunities for hearing about, visiting, and participating in farm activities. The American Kennel Club sponsors clubs dedicated to particular breeds. These clubs usually have educational programs on raising and breeding animals.
• Raising pets is a good introduction to the skills you need for this career. Learning how to care for, feed, and house a pet give you basic knowledge of working with animals.

production work with chickens, turkeys, geese, or ducks.

Education and Training

Classes in mathematics, biology, chemistry, and mechanics will pre-pare you for a future career in animal breeding.

Many animal breeders and technicians learn their skills on the job, but many colleges now offer two-year programs in animal science or

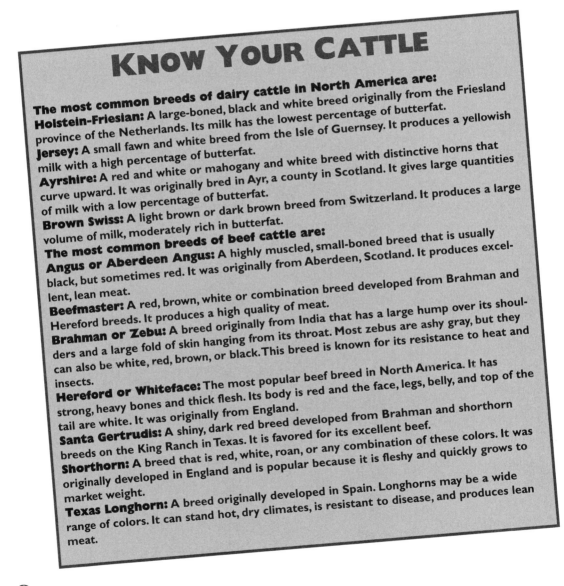

KNOW YOUR CATTLE

The most common breeds of dairy cattle in North America are:

Holstein-Friesian: A large-boned, black and white breed originally from the Friesland province of the Netherlands. Its milk has the lowest percentage of butterfat.

Jersey: A small fawn and white breed from the Isle of Guernsey. It produces a yellowish milk with a high percentage of butterfat.

Ayrshire: A red and white or mahogany and white breed with distinctive horns that curve upward. It was originally bred in Ayr, a county in Scotland. It gives large quantities of milk with a low percentage of butterfat.

Brown Swiss: A light brown or dark brown breed from Switzerland. It produces a large volume of milk, moderately rich in butterfat.

The most common breeds of beef cattle are:

Angus or Aberdeen Angus: A highly muscled, small-boned breed that is usually black, but sometimes red. It was originally from Aberdeen, Scotland. It produces excellent, lean meat.

Beefmaster: A red, brown, white or combination breed developed from Brahman and Hereford breeds. It produces a high quality of meat.

Brahman or Zebu: A breed originally from India that has a large hump over its shoulders and a large fold of skin hanging from its throat. Most zebus are ashy gray, but they can also be white, red, brown, or black. This breed is known for its resistance to heat and insects.

Hereford or Whiteface: The most popular beef breed in North America. It has strong, heavy bones and thick flesh. Its body is red and the face, legs, belly, and top of the tail are white. It was originally from England.

Santa Gertrudis: A shiny, dark red breed developed from Brahman and shorthorn breeds on the King Ranch in Texas. It is favored for its excellent beef.

Shorthorn: A breed that is red, white, roan, or any combination of these colors. It was originally developed in England and is popular because it is fleshy and quickly grows to market weight.

Texas Longhorn: A breed originally developed in Spain. Longhorns may be a wide range of colors. It can stand hot, dry climates, is resistant to disease, and produces lean meat.

animal husbandry (the breeding and care of farm animals). Students learn about feeds and feeding, agricultural equipment, and breeding techniques. You also study farm management and animal health. A high school diploma is almost always needed before you can enter these programs.

Earnings

The salaries of animal breeders and technicians depend on who the employer is, your educational and agricultural background, the kind of animals you work with, and the area where you work. Starting salaries for technicians range from $15,000 to $26,000 a year or more. In addition, many technicians receive food and housing. Starting salaries for animal breeders with bachelor's degrees are about $27,600.

Outlook

Technicians and breeders who have specialized skills and

FOR MORE INFO

This organization distributes public information nationally. It participates in legislative efforts and is the industry liaison for the beef cattle business.
National Cattlemen's Association
PO Box 3469
Englewood, CO 80155
Tel: 303-694-0305

The AKC is the national authority on dog breeding and pedigrees.
American Kennel Club
51 Madison Avenue
New York, NY 10010
Web: http://www.akc.org/akc

American Society of Animal Science
1111 N. Dunlap Avenue
Savoy, IL 61874
Tel: 217-356-3182
Web: http://www.asas.org/

degrees from technical programs will find the most job opportunities. It is becoming more and more difficult for small farms to make a profit, so animal breeders and technicians will find most employment opportunities with large, corporate farms.

Animal Caretakers

Beginnings

The Society for the Prevention of Cruelty to Animals was the first institution to specifically focus on the humane treatment of animals. It was founded in England in 1824. In the United States, the American Humane Association was founded in 1916 to work with the animals used in the war effort. These organizations were concerned with helping animals used for labor and as a food source. The first law protecting animals in the United States was passed in 1873, but changes in animal treatment and rights happened slowly throughout the first part of the 20th century. During the ecology movement in the late 1960s and early 1970s, more attention became focused on the rights and the needs of wildlife and domestic animals.

What Animal Caretakers Do

Animal caretakers provide direct, physical care to animals. They keep track of the animals' general health and clean their surroundings. They work at pet stores, kennels, stables, animal shelters, zoos, aquariums, laboratories, veterinary facilities, and animal experimentation labs. Some animal caretakers work for the federal government (such as the Department of Agriculture and the Centers for Disease Control) and state and local parks. There are many different kinds of animal caretakers. For example, *veterinary assistants* usually work with dogs and cats. *Wildlife shelter workers* work with all sorts of wild animals, from birds to bears.

Generally, animal caretakers feed the animals, clean their living spaces, exercise them, make notes and reports on the animals, and give attention and affection. They are trained to examine animals for

An animal caretaker grooms a llama. Grooming is an important part of keeping animals healthy.

Mathew Hohmann

signs of illness, such as lack of appetite, fatigue, sores, and behavior changes. Animal caretakers keep the animals' living areas clean and safe. They provide stimulating activities, called enrichment activities, for the animals, such as playing with them or walking them.

In some jobs, animal caretakers take on greater responsibilities as they get more experience. They might give medication, trim nails or beaks, and train animals. Some caretakers do clerical or administrative work, such as screening people who want to buy or adopt a pet, writing care plans or reports, or talking with the animals' owners. The main responsibility

EXPLORING

• If your family has a pet, offer to take responsibility for its care, including feeding, exercising, and grooming.

• Volunteer to work at animal shelters, rescue centers, sanctuaries, zoos, or aquariums.

• Start a pet walking or sitting service in your neighborhood. Be sure to only take on the number and kinds of animals you know you can handle.

of animal caretakers, though, is to take care of the animals.

Education and Training

To work as an animal caretaker, you must graduate from high school. In high school you should take classes in anatomy and physiology, science, and health. Any knowledge of animal breeding, behavior, and health will also be helpful.

There are two-year educational programs in animal health. Graduates from these programs usually go on to work in veterinary practices, shelters, zoos and aquariums, pharmaceutical companies, and laboratory research facilities. A bachelor's degree in biology, zoology, or an animal-related field is required for some positions, especially those in zoos and aquariums. Some technicians may need a license (available through the American

Association for Laboratory Animal Science).

Earnings

Animal caretakers earn an average of $15,000 a year, although the pay can range from less

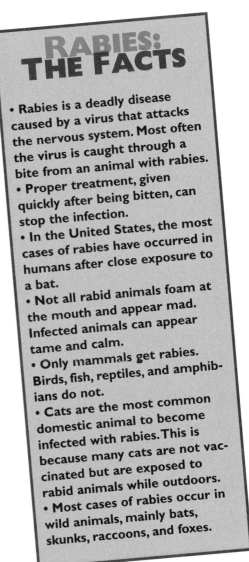

RABIES: THE FACTS

• Rabies is a deadly disease caused by a virus that attacks the nervous system. Most often the virus is caught through a bite from an animal with rabies.
• Proper treatment, given quickly after being bitten, can stop the infection.
• In the United States, the most cases of rabies have occurred in humans after close exposure to a bat.
• Not all rabid animals foam at the mouth and appear mad. Infected animals can appear tame and calm.
• Only mammals get rabies. Birds, fish, reptiles, and amphibians do not.
• Cats are the most common domestic animal to become infected with rabies. This is because many cats are not vaccinated but are exposed to rabid animals while outdoors.
• Most cases of rabies occur in wild animals, mainly bats, skunks, raccoons, and foxes.

than $11,000 a year to more than $24,000. Most positions require little training and as a result offer low salaries. Dog walkers charge between $5 and $12 for each dog.

Outlook

The animal care field keeps growing. More and more people are becoming pet owners, so there is more need for veterinary care, boarding facilities, and grooming and pet shops. Much of the work is part-time. Many employers depend on charitable donations for funding and rely on volunteer labor, so competition is high for paid positions. The most desired positions are in zoos, aquariums, and wildlife rehabilitation centers, but those jobs are the hardest to find.

RELATED JOBS

Animal Shelter Employees
Animal Trainers
Aquarists
Horse Grooms
Pet Groomers
Pet Sitters
Zookeepers

FOR MORE INFO

For information on programs in veterinary technology, contact:
American Veterinary Medical Association
1931 North Meacham Road, Suite 100
Schaumburg, IL 60173-4360
Tel: 847-925-8070 or 800-248-2862
Web: http://www.avma.org

For information about animal laboratory work and certification programs, contact:
American Association for Laboratory Animal Science
9190 Crestwyn Hills Drive
Memphis, TN 38125
Tel: 901-754-8620
Email: info@aalas.org
Web: http://www.aalas.org/

The American Boarding Kennels Association offers several educational programs and publications for members, such as The Pet Services Journal *and* Boarderline *(a newsletter).*
American Boarding Kennels Association
4575 Galley Road, Suite 400A
Colorado Springs, CO 80915
Tel: 719-591-1113
Web: http://www.abka.com

Animal Shelter Workers

The First SPCA

The first American Society for the Prevention of Cruelty to Animals (SPCA) was started in 1866 through the efforts of Henry Bergh and other early crusaders for animal welfare. Not long after, Caroline Earle White and the Women's SPCA of Pennsylvania started the first truly humane animal shelter. Because of these two events, careers in animal shelter work began. Over the years, the focus of animal shelter work has changed from animal control to the welfare and humane treatment of animals.

What Animal Shelter Workers Do

Animal shelter workers work in nonprofit organizations that protect animals and promote animal welfare. Most shelter workers care for small domestic animals, such as cats, dogs, and rabbits, but employees at some shelters also work with horses, goats, pigs, and other larger domestic animals.

Kennel attendants work most closely with the shelter animals. In addition to handling the animals, kennel attendants check the health of animals, refer them for treatment when necessary, and keep records on them. Experienced attendants may be trained to give shots or medications under the supervision of a veterinarian. *Adoption counselors* screen applicants who wish to adopt animals from the shelter. They must have good communication and judgment skills.

Animal control workers respond to calls about neglected or lost animals. They rescue injured animals, control stray and potentially dangerous animals wandering at large, and bring lost pets to an animal shelter where their owners can reclaim them. They sometimes work with local agencies, such as social services or law enforcement to protect both people and animals.

Humane investigators follow up on reports of animal abuse and neglect. They interview witnesses and owners who are accused of mistreatment. If investigators find that there has been abuse or neglect, they may call the police or take the animal away. Humane investigators also rescue stray or injured animals and take them to the shelter.

Humane educators work at the shelter and in the community, teaching about humane treatment of animals. They travel to schools, clubs, and community organizations to talk about animal treatment, animal rights, and other issues. They hand out educational materials and arrange tours of the shelter.

Shelter managers hire, train, and supervise staff and oversee the maintenance of

EXPLORING

• Public libraries have excellent books that give a detailed look into the world of animal shelters and humane societies.

• If you want to learn more about animal shelter work, contact a local shelter to inquire about humane education presentations that are scheduled in the community. You might attend these education sessions or an open house at the shelter.

• Some shelters might agree to allow you to spend a day following or working with a kennel worker.

• Volunteering at a shelter is the best way to learn about careers in animal shelters. Shelters usually welcome volunteers who are considering future careers involving animals.

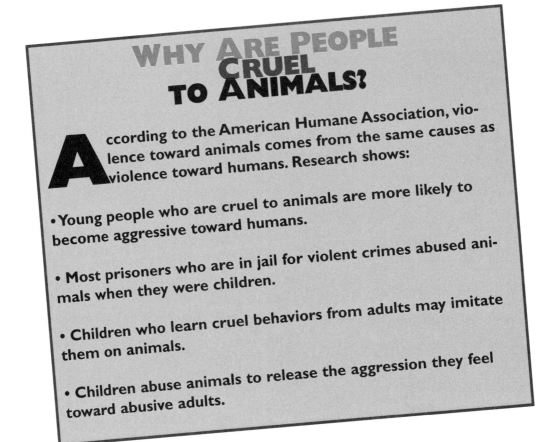

WHY ARE PEOPLE CRUEL TO ANIMALS?

According to the American Humane Association, violence toward animals comes from the same causes as violence toward humans. Research shows:

• Young people who are cruel to animals are more likely to become aggressive toward humans.

• Most prisoners who are in jail for violent crimes abused animals when they were children.

• Children who learn cruel behaviors from adults may imitate them on animals.

• Children abuse animals to release the aggression they feel toward abusive adults.

the property and equipment. *Shelter administrators* are responsible for the overall operation of the shelter. They select and hire shelter managers, humane educators, and humane investigators. They raise funds, attend community events, and recruit new members.

Education and Training

You need a high school diploma or GED to work as a kennel attendant or adoption counselor. Classes in anatomy and biology help prepare you for working with animals. Shelter managers are frequently required to have

a college degree, although experienced veterinary or shelter
workers may be promoted into
the position. Shelter administrators usually need a bachelor's
degree and experience in business or shelter management.

Earnings

Salaries vary widely for animal
shelter employees. Senior level
managers and executive directors can earn, in some cases,
over $100,000 a year. A middle
manager's salary is about
$10,000 to $50,000. Full-time
kennel workers and adoption
counselors earn starting
salaries around $9,500 a year.

Outlook

Employment of animal shelter
workers should remain steady
through 2008. There will be
good jobs available for kennel
workers due to the high
turnover that results from hard
work and low pay. According to
the Humane Society of the
United States, there are
between 4,000 and 6,000 animal shelters in this country.

FOR MORE INFO

*For information on animal welfare topics,
contact:*

The American Humane Association
63 Inverness Drive East
Englewood, CO 80112
Tel: 303-792-9900
Email: apinfo@americanhumane.org
Web: http://www.americanhumane.org

**The American Society for the
Prevention of Cruelty to Animals**
424 East 92nd Street
New York, NY 10128-6804
Web: http://www.aspca.org

**The Humane Society of the
United States**
2100 L Street, NW
Washington, DC 20037
Web: http://www.hsus.org

**The World Society for the
Protection of Animals**
PO Box 190
Boston, MA 02130
Tel: 617-522-7000
Web: http://way.net/wspa

RELATED JOBS

Animal Caretakers
Animal Handlers
Pet Groomers
Pet Sitters
Veterinary Technicians
Zookeepers

Animal Trainers

Most animal trainers use a method called *operant conditioning.* Operant conditioning teaches animals a particular behavior by offering a *positive reinforcer.* A positive reinforcer can be a treat, a toy, a back scratch, or anything that encourages an animal to repeat the desired behavior. For example, when you teach a dog to sit, you can reward its obedience with a treat or by saying "good dog!" Humans learn by operant conditioning, too. When your parents give you money (a positive reinforcer) for mowing the lawn, you are likely to mow the lawn again.

What Animal Trainers Do

Animal trainers teach animals to obey commands, to compete in shows or races, or to perform tricks to entertain audiences. They train dogs to protect property or work in law enforcement or to act as guides for people with disabilities. Animal trainers may specialize in training one kind of animal or they may work with several types.

There are many animals that can be trained, but the same techniques generally are used to train all of them. Animal trainers use a program of repetition and reward to teach animals to behave in a certain consistent way. To do this, they first look at the animal's temperament, ability, and aptitude to see if it is trainable. Then they decide what methods to use to train it. They offer rewards, such as food treats or praise, to gradually teach the animal to obey commands. Animal trainers also feed, exercise,

An animal trainer rewards her student for successfully completing a task.

Mathew Hohmann

groom, and take general care of the animals they train.

One of the most important and common examples of animal training is the companion animal to people with disabilities. These dogs are trained with several hundred verbal commands. They must be able to walk their companions around obstacles on the sidewalk. They must be able to read traffic lights and to cross at the green, and only after traffic has cleared. Very few dogs pass the difficult companion dog training program. Dogs are now trained not only to help those who have visual impairments, but also people who use wheelchairs, who have hearing impairments, or who have other physical disabilities.

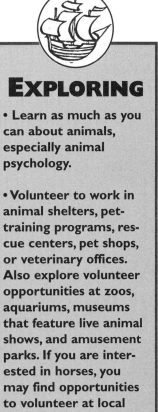

EXPLORING

• Learn as much as you can about animals, especially animal psychology.

• Volunteer to work in animal shelters, pet-training programs, rescue centers, pet shops, or veterinary offices. Also explore volunteer opportunities at zoos, aquariums, museums that feature live animal shows, and amusement parks. If you are interested in horses, you may find opportunities to volunteer at local stables.

Animals have been helping people for hundreds of years. St. Bernards have helped in search and rescue missions in the Swiss Alps for more than 300 years. German shepherds were used in Germany after World War I to guide blind veterans.

Dorothy Eustis, after visiting the program in Germany, started the first American program for training guide dogs, called the Seeing Eye, in 1929. Eustis based the training program on the one that she visited and inspired others to start similar programs. The Seeing Eye still has one facility in the United States, in Morristown, New Jersey, but there are now dozens of programs for the training of guide dogs for people with visual impairments and other physical disabilities.

Training Helper Dogs: It takes about six months to train guide dogs for the blind. After they master basic obedience and get used to the shoulder harness, the dogs learn to follow basic directions (forward, right, and left), to stop at curbs, to cross streets, and to lead their owners around hazards. The dog trainer also works with the new owner, usually for about a month. Together, they work with the dog and learn to use elevators, revolving doors, subway stations, and trains and buses.

Animal trainers usually specialize with one kind of animal. *Dog trainers* train dogs in companion programs, for police work, for performance in the entertainment industry, or to protect private property. *Horse trainers* train horses for riding or harness, or for shows, police work, or the highly specialized field of racehorse training.

Education and Training

There are no special educational requirements for jobs in animal training. A few positions require a college degree. Animal trainers in circuses and the entertainment field are sometimes required to study animal psychology. Zoo and aquarium animal trainers usually must have a B.S. or B.A. degree in a field related to animal management or animal physiology. Trainers of companion dogs for people with disabilities prepare for their work in a three-year course of study at special schools.

Earnings

Salaries for animal trainers range from $10,000 to $100,000 a year, depending on the type of training. Most jobs are low paying, averaging between minimum wage ($5.15 an hour) and $10 an hour. A few specialists, such as those who work with dolphins in aquariums, can earn in the mid-$20,000 range, but very few earn much more. Racehorse trainers earn about $35 to $50 a day for each horse, plus 10 percent of any money the horses win in races. Show horse trainers may earn as much as $30,000 to $35,000 a year.

Outlook

There is not a great demand for animal trainers. Most employers don't need large staffs of trainers. This field is expected to decline through the year 2008. Some openings may be created as zoos and aquariums expand or add more animal shows to make more money.

FOR MORE INFO

For information on careers, contact:
American Zoo and Aquarium Association
Conservation Center
8403 Colesville Road, Suite 710
Silver Spring, MD 20910-3314
Tel: 301-562-0777
Web: http://www.aza.org/

Canine Companions for Independence
National Headquarters
PO Box 446
Santa Rosa, CA 95402-0446
Tel: 800-572-2275 Voice/TTD
Web: http://www.caninecompanions.org/

Delta Society
289 Perimeter Road East
Renton, WA 98055-1329
Tel: 800-869-6898
Web: http://www2.deltasociety.org

Dogs for the Deaf, Inc.
10175 Wheeler Road
Central Point, OR 97502
Tel: 541-826-9220 Voice/TTD
Web: http://www.dogsforthedeaf.org/

Aquarists

What Aquarists Do

Aquarists (pronounced, like "aquarium," with the accent on the second syllable) work for aquariums, oceanariums, and marine research institutes. Their job duties are similar to zookeepers'. Aquarists feed fish, maintain exhibits, and do research. They work on breeding, conservation, and educational programs.

Aquarists clean and take care of tanks every day. They make sure pumps are working, check water temperatures, clean glass, and sift sand. Some exhibits have to be scrubbed. Aquarists also change water frequently and vacuum tanks routinely. They water plants in any marsh or pond exhibits. Food preparation and feeding are important tasks for aquarists. Some animals eat live food, but others eat cut-up food mixtures, and some need special diets prepared. Those that are on special diets may have to be individually fed.

Shedd Aquarium, Chicago

An aquarist feeds a moray eel in the Shedd Aquarium's (Chicago) Coral Reef Exhibit, a huge circular tank where different kinds of fish are displayed together as in a natural marine community.

Aquarists carefully observe all the animals in their care. They must understand their normal habits, including courtship, mating, feeding, social habits, sleeping, and moving, and be able to judge when something is wrong. Aquarists write daily reports and keep detailed records of animal behavior.

Many aquarists are in charge of collecting and stocking plants and animals for exhibits. They may have to make several trips a year to gather live specimens.

Education and Training

Most aquariums hire aquarists who have a college degree in biological sciences with extra studies in marine and aquatic science. Volunteer work is important

EXPLORING

• Ask your parents to help you set up an aquarium. Do research before you start collecting fish. Learn how to maintain equipment, feed and care for the animals, and provide a healthy environment for them.

• Visit your local zoos and aquariums often. Learn about the various species of aquatic animals and observe how they are exhibited.

preparation for a career as an aquarist. Any experience you can get working directly with animals or fish will give you an advantage over other applicants.

Aquarists must be able to dive to feed fish and maintain tanks and to collect new specimens. You need scuba certification, with a special rescue diver classification, for this job. Employers will expect you to pass a diving physical examination before hiring you as an aquarist.

AQUARIUMS TO VISIT

Most aquariums are arranged so that you can view the aquatic life through windows. There is usually a single tank behind each window. Different types of fish and other animals are separated, each living in their own tanks. Public aquariums usually carry on scientific activities behind the scenes. These activities include maintaining breeding and survival centers for endangered species and gathering important data about the species in their collections. These are some of the more famous aquariums in the United States:

John G. Shedd Aquarium, Chicago
National Aquarium, Baltimore
New York Aquarium, New York City
New England Aquarium, Boston
Steinhart Aquarium, San Francisco
Aquarium of the Americas, New Orleans
Monterey Bay Aquarium, Monterey, California

Oceanariums have huge tanks that allow you to view marine animals from above as well as from the sides. The various kinds of marine animals are not separated, but live together in the same tank. Two of the most popular oceanariums are:
Marine Studios, Marineland, Florida
Miami Seaquarium, Miami, Florida

Earnings

Aquarists earn from $23,000 to $32,000 a year. Aquariums usually offer continuing education opportunities to help you keep up with trends and changes. They also pay travel expenses for any research or collecting expeditions.

Outlook

In the next ten years, there will be little change in the number of job openings for aquarists. Some zoos have begun to add aquariums to their exhibits, but the number of aquariums is small compared to the number of people who apply for aquarist jobs.

FOR MORE INFO

Your local aquarium is a good place to start for specific information about aquarists. The American Zoo and Aquarium Association Web site has articles on careers in aquatic and marine science.

American Zoo and Aquarium Association
Department of Education
8403 Colesville Road, Suite 710
Silver Spring, MD 20910
Tel: 301-562-0777
Web: http://www.aza.org

This organization has information on schools, internships, and job opportunities.
American Institute of Biological Sciences
1444 Eye Street, NW, Suite 200
Washington, DC 20005
Tel: 202-628-1500
Web: http://www.aibs.org/

Reading Room

The Ocean Book: Aquarium and Seaside Activities and Ideas for All Ages by the Center for Environmental Education (John Wiley & Sons, 1989).

Setting Up Your First Aquarium (Fish--Keeping & Breeding in Captivity) by Herbert R. Axelrod (Chelsea House Publishers, 1998).

Sea Searcher's Handbook: Activities from the Monterey Bay Aquarium (Monterey Bay Aquarium Press, 1996).

RELATED JOBS

Animal Caretakers
Animal Trainers
Pet Shop Workers
Veterinarians
Veterinary Technicians
Zoo and Aquarium Curators
Zookeepers
Zoologists

Biologists

Activities for Budding Biologists

If you have one of these hobbies, you may have a future as a biologist:

Birdwatching

Collecting butterflies and other insects

Gardening

Microscope study

Raising or caring for animals

Watching nature shows

Visiting nature preserves

Going to the zoo

What Biologists Do

Biologists study how plants and animals grow and reproduce. Sometimes called *biological scientists* or *life scientists,* they often have other job titles because they specialize in one area of biology. *Botanists,* for example, study different types of plants. *Zoologists* study different types of animals. Biologists study living things, while chemists, physicists, and geologists study nonliving matter like rocks and chemicals.

Biologists may do their research in the field or in the laboratory. Their exact job responsibilities vary depending on their area of interest. For example, *aquatic biologists* study plants and animals that live in water. They may do much of their research on a boat studying the water temperature, amount of light, salt levels, and other environmental conditions in the ocean. They then observe how fish and other plants and animals react to these environments.

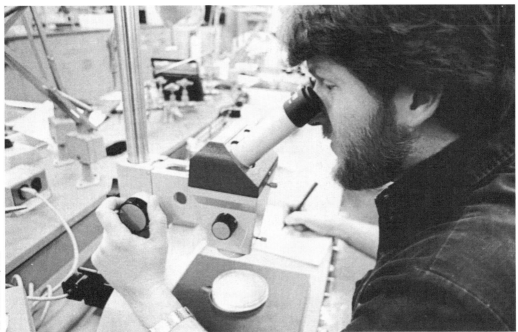

Val von Schacht, UIC

A biologist examines a specimen under a microscope.

No matter what type of research biologists do, they must keep careful records to note all procedures and results. Because biologists may sometimes work with dangerous chemicals and other materials, they always must take safety precautions and carefully follow each step in an experiment.

Some biologists advise businesses and governmental agencies. Others inspect foods and other products. Many biologists write articles for scientific journals. Some may also teach at schools or universities.

EXPLORING

• You can learn about the work of biologists at school field trips to federal or private laboratories and research centers.
• Visit your local museums of natural history or science, aquariums, and zoos.
• Many park districts offer classes and field trips to help you explore plant and animal life.

WHAT DO MICROBIOLOGISTS DO?

Microbiologists are scientists who study bacteria, viruses, molds, algae, yeasts, and other organisms of microscopic size. They study the form and structure of these microorganisms, how they reproduce, and how they affect other living things, such as humans, animals, and plants. Microbiologists work in laboratories at universities, research facilities, and medical institutions, such as hospitals.

Medical microbiologists diagnose, treat, and prevent disease. They use blood and tissue samples from patients and try to find the microbes that cause illness, called pathogens. Clinical microbiologists also try to diagnose and prevent disease. Microbiologists' research has helped to prevent the spread of many diseases, including typhoid fever, influenza, measles, polio, whooping cough, and smallpox. Today, microbiologists are trying to find cures for such diseases as AIDS, cancer, cystic fibrosis, and Alzheimer's disease.

Many microbiologists work in the food industry. They identify pathogens in restaurant kitchens or in processed food that cause salmonella food poisoning. Microbiologists have identified many microorganisms useful to humans. Such microorganisms have been used in the making of food, such as cheese, bread, and tofu. Others are used to preserve food and tenderize meat. Flavors, colors, and added vitamins are all made from microbes.

Microbiologists also work in industry. They make sure manufactured goods are safe. In the pharmaceutical industry, they develop new drugs, such as antibiotics. Microbiologists also test new drugs and cosmetics. They develop new products, such as biological washing detergents. Some microbiologists work for water companies or environmental agencies. They test the quality of water.

Education and Training

If you are thinking about a career in biology, you should plan to take high school courses in biology, chemistry, mathematics, physics, and a foreign language. After high school, you must go to college. During college, you will take more advanced courses in biology, math, chemistry, and physics. Then you choose a specialty. Specialties include microbiology, bacteriology, botany, ecology, or anatomy. Most successful biologists also have a master's degree or a doctorate in biology or in a related field.

Earnings

The average salary for a biologist ranges from $28,000 to more than $68,000 a year. Government biologists with bachelor's degrees earn salaries of about $48,600 a year.

Outlook

There should be plenty of jobs for skilled biologists in the next decade. There is a large num-

FOR MORE INFO

For information about a career as a biologist, contact:
American Institute of Biological Sciences
1444 I Street, NW, Suite 200
Washington, DC 20005
Web: http://www.aibs.org

For a career brochure and career-related articles, contact:
American Physiological Society
Education Office
9650 Rockville Pike
Bethesda, MD 20814-3991
Web: http://www.faseb.org/aps

For information on careers and educational resources, contact:
American Society for Microbiology
Office of Education and
Training—Career Information
1752 N Street, NW
Washington, DC 20036
Web: http://www.asmusa.org

ber of people in this profession, so those with the most education and training will have the best opportunities for jobs. Discoveries in genetics, leading to new drugs, improved crops, and medical treatments should open new opportunities.

Farmers

Farming Facts

In colonial America, almost 95 percent of the population were farmers. They planted corn, wheat, flax, and tobacco. Livestock, including hogs, cattle, sheep, and goats were imported from Europe. Farmers raised hay to feed livestock and just enough other crops to supply their families with a balanced diet throughout the year.

Over one-half of the world's population is still engaged in farming today.

In the United States, farm employment dropped from 9.9 million in 1950 to 2.9 million in 1997.

What Farmers Do

Farmers grow crops, such as peanuts, corn, wheat, cotton, fruits, or vegetables. They also raise cattle, pigs, sheep, chickens, and turkeys for food and keep herds of dairy cattle for milk. Throughout the early history of the United States, farming was a family affair. Today, however, family farms are disappearing. Most large farms are now run by agricultural corporations.

Farmers need good soil and a lot of water for their crops and animals. They need to know how to bring water to their plants (irrigation) and add rich nutrients (fertilizer) to the soil. They also need to know how to keep their animals and crops healthy. They must control insects and diseases that will damage or destroy crops or livestock. They also must provide proper care, such as clean, warm shelters, proper food, and special breeding programs.

An organic farmer windrows wheat on his farm in Minnesota.

Livestock farmers buy calves from ranchers who breed and raise them. They feed and fatten young cattle and often raise their own corn and hay to lower feeding costs. They need to be familiar with cattle diseases and proper methods of feeding. They provide their cattle with fenced pasturage and adequate shelter from rough weather. *Sheep ranchers* raise sheep primarily for their wool. Large herds are maintained on rangeland in the western states. *Dairy farmers* are mostly concerned with producing high-grade milk, but they also raise corn and grain to feed their animals. Dairy animals must be milked twice every day. Farmers clean stalls and barns by washing, sweeping, and sterilizing milking equipment with boiling water. *Poultry farmers* usually do

EXPLORING

Organizations such as 4-H and the National Future Farmers of America offer good opportunities for learning about, visiting, and participating in farming activities.

4-H Clubs
1400 Independence Ave., SW
Stop 2225
Washington, DC
20250-2225
Web: http://www.
4h-usa.org/

National Future
Farmers of America
6060 FFA Drive
PO Box 68960
Indianapolis, IN 46268-0960
Web: http://www.ffa.org/

not hatch their own chicks but buy them from commercial hatcheries. The primary duty of poultry farmers is to keep their flocks healthy. They provide shelter from the chickens' natural enemies and from extreme weather conditions. The shelters are kept extremely clean, because diseases can spread through a flock rapidly. Some poultry farmers raise chickens to be sold as broilers or fryers. Others specialize in the production of eggs. *Beekeepers* set up and manage bee hives. They harvest and sell honey and also cultivate bees for lease to farmers to help pollinate their crops.

Education and Training

Courses in mathematics and science, especially chemistry, earth science, and botany, are important. Accounting, bookkeeping, and computer courses are also very helpful.

After high school, enroll in either a two-year or a four-year course of study in a college of agriculture. For a person with no farm experience, a bachelor's degree in agriculture is essential.

Some universities offer advanced studies in horticulture, animal science, agronomy,

MMMM GOOD!

What do livestock eat? Animals need basic nutrients, such as proteins, carbohydrates, fats, minerals, and vitamins. Specially prepared feeds and roughage, such as hay, supply farm animals with these nutrients. Here's what goes into animal feeds:

- Pasturage (growing grasses, alfalfa, clover)
- Grains
- Hay
- Silage (pasturage and grains stored in airtight structures called silos and allowed to ferment)
- High-protein concentrates (soybean meal, cottonseed oil, blood meal, and bone meal)
- High-carbohydrate concentrates (corn, sorghum, molasses, and dehydrated potatoes)
- Food additives (hormones, antibiotics, vitamins, and minerals)
- By-products from packinghouses, fruit and vegetable processing plants, breweries, distilleries, and paper mills

and agricultural economics. Most students in agricultural colleges also take courses in farm management, business, finance, and economics.

Earnings

Farmers' incomes change from year to year depending on weather, the condition of their farm machinery, the demand for their crops and livestock, and the costs of feed, land, and equipment. The 1998 USDA *Agriculture Fact Book* reported that the average farm household income was $50,360. The same survey showed that 6 percent of the farmers had negative household income.

Outlook

The *Occupational Outlook Handbook* says there were nearly 1.5 million farmers in 1998. Because farming is such a risky business, those entering the career cannot make it without family support or financial aid. Reports show that the number of farmers or farm laborers is decreasing. Rising costs and the

FOR MORE INFO

The Farm Bureau hosts youth conferences and other events for those interested in farming.

American Farm Bureau Federation
225 Touhy Avenue
Park Ridge, IL 60068
Tel: 847-685-8896
Web: http://www.fb.org

National Council of Farmer Cooperatives
50 F Street, NW, Suite 900
Washington, DC 20001
Tel: 202-626-8700
Web: http://www.ncfc.org

U.S. Department of Agriculture
Higher Education Program
14th Street and Independence, SW
Washington, DC 20250
Tel: 202-720-2791
Web: http://www.usda.gov/

trend toward larger farms are forcing out the small farmers.

Despite the great difficulty in becoming a farmer today, there are many agriculture-related careers that involve people with farm production, marketing, management, and agribusiness.

Horse Grooms

Classic Horse Tales

The beauty and power of horses have captured the imagination of story-tellers for centuries. Here are some classic tales to read:

The Black Stallion
by Walter Farley

Misty of Chincoteague
by Marguerite Henry

My Friend Flicka
by Mary O'Hara

Man O'War
by Walter Farley

Black Beauty
by Anna Sewell

What Horse Grooms Do

Horses are valued for their speed, grace, and beauty. They are bred and raced at stables and racetracks all over the country. Owners and trainers invest a great deal of time and effort to make sure their horses are well cared for. *Horse grooms* are an important part of the team they hire to do this.

Grooms have many daily duties. They must feed and water each horse under their care. Depending on its size and age, a horse can eat as much as 20 pounds of hay and 12 pounds of grain a day, and drink more than 12 gallons of water. Horses also need some salt every day. Many take extra protein, vitamins, and minerals to balance their diets. Grooms prepare the feed and make sure each horse gets what it needs to stay healthy. This is especially important for racing horses, who must be in top shape.

Horses also must get a certain amount of exercise—at least an hour per day. Other track workers—specially trained exercisers—are responsible for this. After exercise, or after a race, workers called *hotwalkers* walk a horse until it cools down.

The groom then bathes, brushes, and combs the horse to keep its coat healthy and help improve muscle tone. The groom uses a variety of tools for this job. Curry combs, dandy brushes, and body brushes help loosen dirt and dead hair, cleaning the horse's coat. A special comb may be used for its mane and tail. A hoof pick cleans the bottom of its feet. Grooms help groom horses, but they are not responsible for maintaining horseshoes. This is the work of a trained technician called a *farrier.*

Grooms are important to the running of a stable or racetrack. Because they spend so much time with the horses, grooms often are the first to recognize when something is wrong. They notice when a horse stops eating properly, or "goes off its feed," or when it's lame and may have been injured during regular exercise or a race. Finding these problems early is critical, both for the horse's health and for its ability to race.

EXPLORING

• Take riding lessons.

• Spend time at stables to watch and learn about the care of horses. You may be able to volunteer or work part-time as a stable helper. This type of work is not always pleasant—you will probably have to shovel manure and clean stables—but you will learn a lot from being around horses and their grooms.

• Ask your librarian to help you find books on horses and racing. Read about horse anatomy, different breeds of horses, how to care for horses, the racing business, and types of races.

know how to tell when their horses are suffering physical problems, and when they need medical attention.

State racing commissions require that all track workers be licensed. To be licensed, you must provide certain personal information and be at least 16 years old. You must be able to prove you have been hired by a trainer, and the trainer must sign the license application. When a groom stops working for a particular trainer, the racing commission must be notified.

Education and Training

A high school education is helpful for horse groom careers, but not strictly required. Trainers prefer to hire grooms who know a little about biology or physiology. Biology and physiology are important because grooms must

Earnings

Horse grooms are paid based on how many horses they take care of, so their wages vary. An average groom is responsible for four to five horses. Most grooms are paid at least $75 per week per horse, but there is no minimum wage. The average per horse rate is approximately $100 per week, or about $24,000 a year.

Full-time horse grooms who work at race tracks often live in quarters on site. Grooms sometimes are "staked," or offered a percentage of their horses' winnings, since successful racing depends a great deal on how well cared for the horses are. Grooms who work with racing horses travel to different race tracks with the trainer and the rest of the team involved in preparing the horse for a race.

Outlook

Opportunities in this field should grow about as fast as other occupations over the next few years. Horses require daily attention—feeding, bathing, and brushing—and stalls must be kept clean. These basic needs are the job of the groom, and must be done whether the horse is racing or not. Owners and breeders will continue to require the help of good grooms.

FOR MORE INFO

You can find out more about horse racing from this organization. Their Web site also has links to many other organizations for people who are interested in and work with horses.
Thoroughbred Owners' and Breeders' Association
PO Box 4367
Lexington, KY 40544
Tel: 606-276-2291
Web: http://www.toba.org

This organization puts out a monthly newsletter called Equine Care Watch Bulletin, *with information about research, legislation, and other horse-care topics.*
National Thoroughbred Racing Association
2343 Alexandria Drive, Suite 210
Lexington, KY 40504
Tel: 606-223-0658
Web: http://www.ntraracing.com

Marine Biologists

Octopus FunFacts

• The largest octopus is the North Pacific Octopus (*Octopus dofleini*). It can grow to over 30 feet and weighs more than 100 pounds.
• The smallest octopus is the Californian Octopus (*Octopus micropyrsus*). It is only 3/8 inch to 1 inch in length.
• When threatened, octopuses often try to escape by releasing a cloud of purple-black ink to confuse the enemy.

Shark FunFacts

• Slow growing sharks, such as the tope shark and piked dogfish can live more than 40 years.
• Only 32 species of sharks have ever attacked people.
• There are more than 350 species of sharks.
• Sharks eat almost anything, including fishes, crustaceans, mollusks, marine mammals, and other sharks.

What Marine Biologists Do

Marine biologists study the plants and animals that live in oceans. They learn about the tens of thousands of different species that live in salt water.

To study these plants and animals in their natural environment, marine biologists take sea voyages. When they reach their destination, perhaps near a coral reef or other habitat, the scientists dive into the water to collect samples.

Because of the cold temperatures below the surface of the sea, marine biologists must wear wetsuits to keep warm. They use scuba gear to help them breathe under water. They may carry a tool, called a slurp gun, which can suck a fish into a specimen bag without hurting it. While underwater, biologists must be on the lookout for dangerous fish. They take great care not to damage the marine environment.

Marine biologists also gather specimens from tidal pools along the shore. They may collect samples at the same time of day for days at a time. They keep samples from different pools separate and carefully write down the pool's location, the types of specimens taken, and their measurements. It is important to keep accurate records.

After they collect specimens, scientists keep them in a special portable aquarium tank on the ship. After returning to land, sometimes weeks or months later, marine biologists study the specimens in their laboratories. They might check the amount of oxygen in a sea turtle's blood stream to learn how the turtles can stay underwater for so long. Or they might measure the blood chemistry of an arctic fish to discover how it can survive frigid temperatures.

Marine biologists study changing conditions of the ocean, such as temperature or chemicals that have polluted the water. They try to see how those changes affect the plants and animals that live there. If certain species become extinct or are no longer safe to eat, the world's food supply grows smaller.

EXPLORING

• Visit your local aquarium to learn about marine life and about the life of a marine biologist.

• If you live near an ocean you can collect shells and other specimens. Keep a notebook to record details about what you find and where.

• You can begin diving training while in high school. Between the ages of 12 and 15 you can earn a Junior Open Water Diver certification. This allows you to dive in the company of a certified adult. When you turn 15 you can upgrade your certification to Open Water Diver.

• Take up hobbies, such as swimming, boating, snorkeling, or fishing.

• Turtles and fish make good pets for future marine biologists.

Edward Seidel works as a research biologist for the Monterey Bay Aquarium in Monterey, California. He spends some of his hours diving in the bay to observe marine animals. He collects specimens for study and exhibit at the aquarium. He also designs exhibit habitats that will provide the correct nutritional needs. water temperature, pressure, and salt content.

When Ed was in college, he took a biology course where he had to study squids and sea slugs. It was there that he first became interested in marine life.

Then he joined the Peace Corps and went to the Philippines where he did marine fisheries work. Fishermen there had begun to dynamite the waters for fish to get large enough hauls to make a living. Ed helped some of them find other types of fishing work.

After his return to the United States, Ed got his first job at the Monterey Bay Aquarium in their public outreach/educational unit. Ed now does research. He will soon earn his master's degree.

The work of these scientists is also important for improving and managing sport and commercial fishing. Through underwater exploration, these scientists have discovered that the world's coral reefs are being destroyed by humans. They have also charted the migration of whales and counted the decreasing numbers of certain species. They have seen dolphins being caught by accident in tuna fishermen's nets. By telling people their discoveries through written reports and research papers, marine biologists sometimes make important changes in behavior that will help the world.

Education and Training

If you want to be a marine biologist, you should like math and science. Biology, botany, and chemistry classes are important to take in high school. You also should be able to ask questions and solve problems, observe small details carefully, do research, and work out mathematical problems. Although you can get a job as a marine biologist with a bachelor's degree, most marine biologists have a master's or a doctoral degree.

Earnings

Salaries vary depending on how much education and experience you have. The average biologist earns about $36,000 yearly. Those who have doctorates in marine biology can earn as much as $80,000 a year. Senior scientists or full professors at universities can earn more than $100,000 a year.

Outlook

There is a lot of competition for the best jobs in marine biology. Opportunities in research are especially hard to find. If you have an advanced degree and specialized knowledge in mathematics and computer science you will have the best chances for employment. Changes in the earth's environment, such as global warming, will most likely require more research and so create more jobs. Marine biolo-

FOR MORE INFO

For information on careers, contact:
American Society of Limnology and Oceanography
Web: http://www.aslo.org

For links to marine labs, summer intern and course opportunities, and links to career information, visit this Web site:
Marine Biology Web Page
State University of New York
Department of Ecology and Evolution
Stony Brook, New York 11794
Tel: 516-632-8602
Email: levinton@life.bio.sunysb.edu
Web: http://life.bio.sunysb.edu/marinebio/mbweb.html

For information on diving instruction and certification, contact:
Professional Association of Diving Instructors
30151 Tomas Street
Rancho Santa Margarita, CA 92688-2125
Tel: 949-858-7234
Web: http://www.padi.com

gists should be able to find jobs managing the world's fisheries, making medicines from marine organisms, and cultivating marine food alternatives, such as seaweed and plankton.

Naturalists

The Beginnings of Conservation

During the 19th century in the United States, many great forests were cut down and huge areas of land were leveled for open-pit mining and quarrying. More disease occurred with the increase of air pollution from the smokestacks of factories, home chimneys, and engine exhaust. At the same time there was a dramatic decrease in populations of elk, antelope, deer, bison, and other animals of the Great Plains. Some types of bear, cougar, and wolf became extinct, as well as several kinds of birds, such as the passenger pigeon. In the latter half of the 19th century, the government set up a commission to develop scientific management of fisheries. It established the first national park (Yellowstone National Park in Wyoming), and set aside the first forest reserves. These early steps led to the modern conservation movement.

What Naturalists Do

Naturalists study the natural world in order to learn the best way to preserve the earth and its living creatures— humans, animals, and plants. They teach the public about the environment and show people what they can do about such hazards as pollution.

Naturalists may work in wildlife museums, private nature centers, or large zoos. Some naturalists work for parks, most of which are operated by state or federal governments. Naturalists also can work as *nature resource managers, wildlife conservationists, ecologists,* and *environmental educators* for many different employers.

Depending on where they work, naturalists may protect and conserve wildlife or particular kinds of land, such as prairie or wetlands. Other naturalists research and carry out plans to restore lands that have been damaged by erosion, fire, or devel-

Thunder Mountain

opment. Some naturalists re-create wildlife habitats and nature trails. They plant trees, for example, or label existing plants. *Fish and wildlife wardens* help regulate populations of fish, hunted animals, and protected animals. They control hunting and fishing and make sure species are thriving but not overpopulating their territories. *Wildlife managers, range managers,* and *conservationists* also maintain the plant and animal life in a certain area. They work in parks or on ranges that have both domestic livestock and wild animals. They test soil and water for nutrients and pollution. They count plant and animal populations each season.

Naturalists do some indoor work. They raise funds for projects, write reports,

EXPLORING

• Visit your local nature centers and park preserves often. Attend any classes or special lectures they offer. There may be opportunities to volunteer to help clean up sites, plant trees, or maintain pathways and trails.
• Hiking, birdwatching, and photography are good hobbies for future naturalists.
• Get to know your local wildlife. What kind of insects, birds, fish, and other animals live in your area? You librarian will be able to help you find books that identify local flora and fauna.

keep detailed records, and write articles, brochures, and newsletters to educate the public about their work. They might campaign for support for protection of an endangered species by holding meetings and hearings. Other public education activities include giving tours and nature walks and holding demonstrations, exhibits, and classes.

Education and Training

Naturalists must have at least a bachelor's degree in biology, zoology, chemistry, botany, natural history, or environmental science. A master's degree is not a requirement, but is useful, and many naturalists have a master's degree in education. Experience gained through summer jobs and volunteer work can be just as important as educational requirements.

Experience working with the public is also helpful.

Earnings

Starting salaries for full-time naturalists range from about

SOME PIONEER NATURALISTS

Ralph Waldo Emerson (1803-1882) was an American philosopher and author. He helped form and promote the philosophy known as Transcendentalism, which emphasizes the spiritual dimension in nature and in all persons.

Henry David Thoreau (1817-1862) was an American author. His *Walden* (1854) is a classic of American literature. It tells about the two years he lived in a small cabin on the shore of Walden Pond near Concord, Massachusetts. In *Walden*, he described the changing seasons and other natural events and scenes that he observed.

Gilbert White (1720-1793) was an English minister. While living and working in his native village of Selborne (southwest of London), White became a careful observer of its natural setting. He corresponded with important British naturalists and eventually published *The Natural History and Antiquities of Selborne*.

$15,000 to $22,000 per year. Some part-time workers, however, make as little as minimum wage ($5.15 per hour). For some positions, housing and vehicles may be provided. Earnings vary for those with added responsibilities or advanced degrees. Field officers and supervisors make between $25,000 and $45,000 a year, and upper management employees can earn between $30,000 and $70,000.

Outlook

In the next decade, the job outlook for naturalists is expected to be only fair, despite the public's increasing environmental awareness. Private nature centers and preserves—where forests, wetlands, and prairies are restored—are continuing to open in the United States, but possible government cutbacks in nature programs may limit their growth. Competition will be quite high, since there are many qualified people entering this field.

FOR MORE INFO

Contact the following organizations for more information on a career as a naturalist:
Bureau of Land Management
U.S Department of the Interior
1849 C Street, Room 406-LS
Washington, DC 20240
Web: http://www.blm.gov/

Environmental Careers Organization
179 South Street
Boston, MA 02111
Web: http://www.eco.org/

This group has an international computer network called EcoNet that features electronic bulletin boards on environmental issues, services, events, news, and job listings.
Institute for Global Communication
18 DeBoom Street
San Francisco, CA 94107
Tel: 415-442-0220
Web: http://www.econet.org

National Wildlife Federation
8925 Leesburg Pike
Vienna, VA 22184
Tel: 718-790-4000
Web: http://www.nwf.org

North American Association for Environmental Education
1825 Connecticut Avenue, NW
Washington, DC 20009-5708
Tel: 202-884-8912
Web: http://naaee.org/

Park Rangers

What Park Rangers Do

Park rangers protect animals and preserve forests, ponds, and other natural resources in state and national parks. They teach visitors about the park by giving lectures and tours. They also enforce rules and regulations to maintain a safe environment for visitors and wildlife.

One of the most important responsibilities park rangers have is safety. Rangers often require visitors to register at park offices so they will know when the visitors are expected to return from a hike or other activity. Rangers are trained in first aid and, if there is an accident, they may have to help visitors who have been injured. Rangers carefully mark hiking trails and other areas to lessen the risk of injuries for visitors and to protect plants and animals.

Rangers help visitors enjoy and learn about parks. They give lectures and provide guided tours of the park, explaining

Richard Frear, National Park Service

Many accidents occur in national parks. For that reason, rangers must be trained in first aid and emergency care.

the park. Then they develop plans to help reduce pollution to make the park a better place for plants, animals, and visitors.

Rangers also do bookkeeping and other paperwork. They issue permits to visitors and keep track of how many people use the park. They also plan recreational activities and decide how to spend the money budgeted to the park.

why certain plants and animals live there. They explain about the rocks and soil in the area and point out important historical sites.

Research and conservation efforts are also a big part of a park ranger's responsibilities. They study wildlife behavior by tagging and following certain animals. They may investigate sources of pollution that come from outside

EXPLORING

• You may be able to volunteer at national, state, or county parks. Universities and conservation organizations often have volunteer groups that work on research activities, study projects, and rehabilitation efforts.

• Get to know your local wildlife. What kind of insects, birds, fish, and other animals live in your area? Your librarian will be able to help you find books that identify local flora and fauna.

PARKS IN DANGER

The National Parks Conservation Association listed the 10 most endangered national parks in 2000. The names of the parks are followed by their major threats.

Yellowstone National Park: Snowmobiles, which cause noise, ground, and air pollution.

Denali National Park: Proposal to open access by snowmobiles. Road and resort development.

Joshua Tree National Park: Proposed landfill for a site 1.5 miles outside the park.

Haleakala National Park: Introduction of non-native organisms that threaten rare plants and animals.

Everglades and Biscayne National Parks, and Big Cypress National Preserve: Damage from water management. Off-road vehicle use. Proposed airport development.

Petrified Forest National Park: Visitors taking an estimated 12 tons of fossilized wood annually.

Stones River National Battlefield: Proposed highway and commercial development.

National Underground Railroad Network to Freedom: Lack of funding for buying private property needed for the preservation of this network of sites.

Great Smoky Mountains National Park: Air pollution from regional power-generating plants and motor vehicles.

Ozarks Scenic Riverways National Park: Mining in the surrounding Mark Twain National Forest.

Education and Training

Park rangers usually have bachelor's degrees in natural resource or recreational resource management. A degree in many other fields is also acceptable, such as biology or ecology. Classes in forestry, geology, outdoor management, history, geography, behavioral sciences, and botany, are helpful.

Without a degree, you need at least three years of experience working in parks or conservation. You must know about protecting plants and animals and enjoy working outdoors. You also need a pleasant personality and the ability to work with many different kinds of people. You should be good at explaining the natural environment and be able to enforce park rules and regulations. Rangers also receive on-the-job training.

Earnings

Rangers in the National Park Service usually earn starting salaries of around $21,000 a year. More experienced or educated rangers earn approximately $32,000 a year. The government may provide housing to park rangers who work in remote areas.

Outlook

The number of people who want to become park rangers has always been far greater than the number of positions available. The National Park Service has reported that as many as 100 people apply for each job opening. This trend should continue into the future, and because of this stiff compe-

FOR MORE INFO

Contact the following groups for more information on a career as a park ranger:

National Parks Conservation Association
1300 19th Street, NW, Suite 300
Washington, DC 20036
Tel: 202-223-6722
Web: http://www.npca.org/

National Recreation and Park Association
22377 Belmont Ridge Road
Ashburn, VA 20148-4510
Tel: 703-858-0784
Web: http://www.nrpa.org

Student Conservation Association
PO Box 550
Charlestown, NH 03603-0550
Tel: 603-543-1700
Web: http://www.sca-inc.org

tition for positions, the job outlook is expected to change little. Besides the National Park Service, there are some job opportunities in other federal land and resource management agencies and similar state and local agencies.

Pet Groomers

What Pet Groomers Do

Pet groomers bathe, trim, shape, brush, and comb animals' coats to make them look good and help them stay healthy. They also clip nails, clean ears, and examine animals for fleas, ticks, and other health problems. Most of a pet groomer's business comes from shaggy, long-haired dogs and dogs with special grooming styles, such as poodles, schnauzers, cocker spaniels, and terriers. Show dogs—dogs that are shown in competition—are groomed frequently.

More and more cats, especially long-haired breeds, are now being taken to pet groomers. The procedure for dogs and cats is essentially the same, although cats do not receive the full bathing treatment given to dogs. Pet groomers first place the animal on a grooming table and steady it with a nylon collar. Some animals are extremely nervous and uncooperative during grooming procedures. If the groomer is unable to calm the animal and gain its trust, he or she may muzzle it. Some pets even have to be tranquilized by a veterinarian for the grooming procedure.

Groomers brush the animals to remove shedding hair and dead skin. The brushing is followed by cutting and shaping, when necessary. The groomer then cleans the animal's ears and trims its nails, taking care not to cut them too short, which is painful and causes bleeding. In the case of dogs, bathing follows. The dog is lowered into a stainless steel tub, sprayed with warm water, scrubbed with a special shampoo, and rinsed. At this point, any special treatments, such as deodorizing or treating ticks or fleas, are completed. Most dogs can be groomed in about 90 minutes. Poodles usually take the longest because of their intricate clipping pattern. Also, shaggier breeds whose coats are badly matted and overgrown can take several hours. Most cats can be groomed in much less time.

Education and Training

There are three basic ways to become a dog groomer. Many groomers teach themselves by reading books on the subject and then practicing on their own and friends' pets. They learn the more compli-

EXPLORING

• Take care of your family pet, including walking, feeding, and grooming.

• Offer to help your friends and neighbors take care of their pets.

• Youth organizations such as the Boy Scouts, Girl Scouts, and 4-H Clubs sponsor projects that give you opportunities to raise and care for animals.

• Volunteer to care for animals at an animal hospital, kennel, pet shop, animal shelter, nature center, or zoo.

• Learn about different breeds of dogs and cats and their special grooming needs.

cated cuts and important safety precautions while working under an experienced groomer. Some groomers begin by working in a veterinarian's office, kennel, or pet shop, and learn on the job. They may begin with shampooing animals and work up to brushing, clipping, and expert trimming. Other groomers enroll in accredited pet grooming schools, where they study bathing, brushing, clipping, the care of the ears and nails, coat and skin conditions, animal anatomy terminology, and sanitation.

Many high school courses are useful to those interested in pet grooming, such as anatomy and physiology, health, science, first aid, business math, English, and psychology. A high school diploma is not required to become a pet groomer, but it is helpful for advancement.

MAGAZINES FOR GROOMERS

Pet Stylist Magazine
International Society of Canine Cosmetologists
2702 Covington Drive
Garland, TX 75040
Web: http://www.petstylist.com

Groom & Board Magazine
H.H. Backer Associates, Inc.
20 E. Jackson Boulevard
Chicago, IL 60604
Tel: 312-663-4040

Groomer to Groomer Magazine
Barkleigh Publications, Inc.
6 State Road, Suite 113
Mechanicsburg, PA 17055
Tel: 717-691-3388

Groomer's Voice Newsletter
National Dog Groomer's Association of America, Inc.
PO Box 101
Clark, PA 16113
Tel: 724-962-2711

Earnings

Groomers who work for a salon or another groomer usually keep 50 to 60 percent of the fees they charge. Pet groomers made an average of $14,300 in 1998, although the top 10 percent earned more than $24,000. Those who own and operate their own grooming services can earn more. Groomers usually buy their own clipping equipment, including barber's shears, brushes, and clippers. A new set of equipment costs around $325.

Outlook

The demand for groomers has grown faster than average, and growth is expected to continue through 2008. The National Dog Groomers Assocation of America says there are more than 30,000 dog groomers and more than 3,000 new groomers will be needed every year during the next decade. Every year more people are keeping dogs and cats as pets, and they are spending more money to pamper them. There will also be opportunities for groomers who are prepared to handle the growing number of nontraditional pets, such as ferrets, birds, and reptiles.

FOR MORE INFO

This organization has information on shows, workshops, and certification test sites and dates. For information and/or a list of dog grooming schools across the country, send a stamped, self-addressed #10 envelope to:
National Dog Groomers Association of America, Inc.
PO Box 101
Clark, PA 16113
Tel: 724-962-2711
Web: http://www.nauticom.net/www/ndga/index.html

For more information about grooming and related professions, contact:
Intergroom
250 East 73rd Street, Suite 4-F
New York, NY 10021-4311
Tel: 212-628-3537
Email: intergroom@aol.com
Web: http://www.intergroom.com/

PetGroomer.com features nearly 800 links to pet grooming career information.
PetGroomer.com
Web: http://www.petgroomer.com

Pet Sitters

What Pet Sitters Do

Pet sitters visit clients' homes to care for their pets. During short, daily visits, pet sitters feed the animals, give them fresh water, play with them, clean up after them, give them medications when needed, and let them in and out of the house for exercise. *Dog walkers* may be responsible only for taking their clients' dogs out for exercise. Pet sitters may also offer overnight services to look after the clients' houses as well as their pets.

Pet sitters let themselves into clients' homes with their own sets of keys and care for the animals while their owners are at work or out of town. They play with and sometimes feed the animals and provide care, attention, and affection at times when the owners cannot. Pet sitters must do some "dirty work," such as cleaning litter boxes and any messes that the animals make. Some pet sitters offer services that may include taking a pet to the vet, grooming the pet, or providing advice.

Pet sitters usually visit clients' homes one to three times per day. Each visit lasts 30 to 60 minutes. Often, pet sitters are responsible for other tasks, such as bringing in the mail and newspapers, watering plants, and making sure the house is securely locked.

Most pet sitters work alone, without co-workers or employees. In addition to caring for animals, pet sitters have to manage their businesses. They have to find new clients, schedule appointments, and give referrals for boarders and vets. Pet sitters also must work weekends and holidays, since those are prime times for pet owners to be away from home.

Education and Training

There are no special education requirements for pet sitting work. Classes in biology, health, accounting, and marketing will be helpful. For this work, experience is the best education. To get experience, volunteer your pet sitting services to your neighbors or call an established pet sitter and ask if you can tag along or even work for a day or two. This is an

EXPLORING

• Offer pet sitting services to neighbors or friends. Start with one or two clients. If you do a good job, they will recommend you to other friends and neighbors. You will get valuable experience in taking care of animals, and you will also learn about running a business.

• There are many books, newsletters, and magazines about pet care. Here are some suggestions:

Pet Sitting for Profit by Patti Moran (IDG Books Worldwide, 1997).

The Professional Pet Sitter by Lori and Scott Mangold (Paws-Itive Press, 1999).

Cat Fancy magazine
Dog Fancy magazine
PO Box 52864
Boulder, CO 80322-2864
Web: http://www.
animalnetwork.com/

Michele Finley is a pet sitter in the Park Slope neighborhood of Brooklyn, New York. "A lot of people seem to think pet sitting is a walk in the park," she says, "and go into it without realizing what it entails."

Finley works directly with the animals from 10:00 AM until 5:00 or 6:00 PM, with no breaks. When she returns home, she will have five to 10 phone messages from clients. She spends part of her evening scheduling and rescheduling appointments; offering advice on feeding, training, and other pet care concerns; and giving referrals for boarders and vets. She works long hours, including holidays, and has to work even when she's not feeling well. Still, Finley likes many things about the job. "Being with the furries all day is the best," she says. She also likes not having to dress up for work and not having to commute to an office.

For those who are thinking about pet sitting, Finley has this advice: "Work for an established pet sitter to see how you like it. It's a very physically demanding job and not many can stand it for long on a full-time basis."

excellent way to learn firsthand the duties of a pet sitter.

Pet Sitters International (PSI) offers four levels of accreditation: Pet Sitting Technician, Advanced Pet Sitting Technician, Master Professional Pet Sitter, and Accredited Pet Sitting Service. Pet sitters complete home study courses in animal nutrition, office procedures, and management. Accreditation is not required, but you are more likely to earn your clients' trust and find new clients if you have earned your accreditation.

Earnings

Pet sitters set their own prices and may charge by the visit, the hour, or the week. They may also charge consultation fees and extra fees on holidays. Generally, pet sitters charge between $8 and $15 a visit (with a visit lasting 30 to 60 minutes).

A few very successful pet sitters earn more than $100,000 per year, while others make only $5,000 a year. Bigger cities offer more clients for pet sitters. Pet sitters usually make around $10,000 in their first five years. After eight years or more they earn around $40,000 a year.

Outlook

Pet sitting businesses are expected to grow rapidly in the next few years. Many pet owners like to use in-home pet sitters instead of boarders and kennels because their pets can stay at home in familiar surroundings, pets aren't exposed to sick animals, and they get daily exercise and individual attention. Since pet sitters' fees are usually about the same as kennels and boarders, pet sitting has become a desirable and cost-effective alternative for pet owners.

FOR MORE INFO

For career and small business information as well as general information about pet sitting, contact:

Pet Sitters International
418 East King Street
King, NC 27021-9163
Tel: 336-983-9222
Web: http://www.petsit.com

National Association of Professional Pet Sitters
1030 15th Street, NW, Suite 870
Washington, DC 20005
Tel: 202-393-3317
Web: http://www.petsitters.org/

Pet Problems

Most pets at some time have parasites, such as fleas, ticks, lice, or mites. Parasites can be extremely irritating to a pet and cause serious skin disorders or even disease. If you notice that a pet in your care scratches frequently or has bald spots or inflammation of the skin, tell the owner right away. Recommend that they take the pet to a veterinarian for diagnosis and treatment.

Veterinarians

What Veterinarians Do

Veterinarians are doctors who treat sick and injured animals and give advice on how to care for and breed healthy animals. Veterinarians treat dogs, cats, and other pets, but some also work with farm and zoo animals.

Most veterinarians work with small animals that people keep as companions, such as dogs, cats, and birds. They perform surgery, treat minor illnesses, and board both sick and healthy animals that need a temporary place to stay. Sometimes they make emergency house calls, but most veterinarians try to keep normal business hours. A number of doctors may work as many as 60 hours a week if emergency health problems occur.

Other veterinarians work with larger animals or may even work with both large animals and small house pets. Some of these doctors specialize in the treatment and care of animals such as horses, cat-

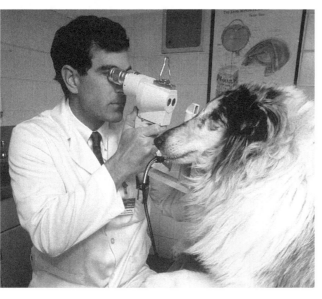

A veterinarian examines a sick collie.

tle, and sheep. Others specialize in treating fish or poultry, such as ducks and geese.

In small towns or in the country, veterinarians may travel long distances to treat animals. Some large cattle ranches or horse farms keep veterinarians on their staff. Most zoos also employ a full-time veterinarian to manage the health care, feeding, and treatment of their entire animal population.

Many veterinarians work as inspectors in the food industry, such as in meat-packing and chicken-processing companies. They examine the meat for signs of disease.

EXPLORING

• You may be able to find volunteer work on farms, in small-animal clinics, pet shops, or animal shelters.

• Extracurricular activities, such as 4-H clubs, offer opportunities to learn about the care of animals.

Education and Training

To set up private practice as a veterinarian, you must have a doctor of veterinary medicine (D.V.M.) degree. You must also pass a state licensing board exam plus one or more national exams. You need at least six years of college after graduation from high school to earn a D.V.M. degree. Most accredited schools of veterinary medicine in the United States offer four-year programs, and most require you to complete at least two years of general college courses before you enter the veterinarian program. Some junior colleges offer preveterinary training.

Many preveterinary students obtain a bachelor's degree from a four-year college before they apply for admission to the D.V.M. degree program. Admission to schools of veterinary medicine is very competitive, and you typically must have grades of "B" or better, especially in the sciences. You

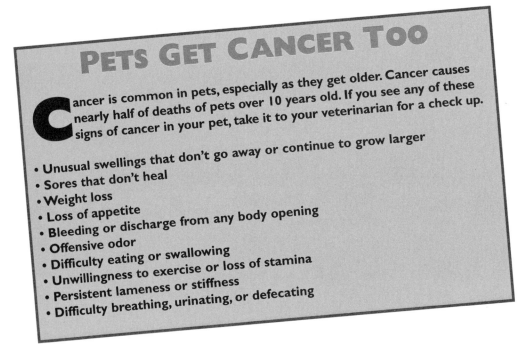

PETS GET CANCER TOO

Cancer is common in pets, especially as they get older. Cancer causes nearly half of deaths of pets over 10 years old. If you see any of these signs of cancer in your pet, take it to your veterinarian for a check up.

- Unusual swellings that don't go away or continue to grow larger
- Sores that don't heal
- Weight loss
- Loss of appetite
- Bleeding or discharge from any body opening
- Offensive odor
- Difficulty eating or swallowing
- Unwillingness to exercise or loss of stamina
- Persistent lameness or stiffness
- Difficulty breathing, urinating, or defecating

must also take the Veterinary Aptitude Test, the Medical College Admission Test, or the Graduate Record Examination. Fewer than half of all applicants are admitted, due to small class sizes and limited facilities.

Earnings

Newly graduated veterinarians employed by the federal government have starting salaries of about $35,800 a year. Average salaries for government veterinarians are $61,600. Veterinarians in private industry average $51,000 a year. Salaries range from $32,000 at the low end to $106,000 at the high end. Veterinarians who specialize in large animal care average $37,500 a year. Those who specialize in small animal care average $36,300 a year.

Outlook

In 1998, about 30 percent of the more than 57,000 veterinarians worked in private clinical practice. The federal government employed about 1,900 veterinarians, mostly in the

FOR MORE INFO

For more information on veterinary careers and how to prepare for them, contact the following organizations:

American Veterinary Medical Association
1930 North Meacham Road, Suite 100
Schaumburg, IL 60173-4360
Attn: Education and Research Division
Web: http://www.avma.org

U.S. Department of Agriculture
Animal and Plant Health
Inspection Service
Butler Square West, 4th Floor
100 North Sixth Street
Minneapolis, MN 55403
Web: http://www.usda.gov

The following Web site offers links to educational and career resources for veterinarians.
NetVet
Web: http://netvet.wustl.edu/vet.htm

Department of Agriculture and the Public Health Service. The rest worked in industry or schools and universities. Employment of veterinarians is expected to grow faster than the average through the year 2008, according to the U.S. Department of Labor.

Veterinary Technicians

What Veterinary Technicians Do

Veterinary technicians help veterinarians care for animals. In clinics or private practices, veterinary technicians help with surgical procedures. They prepare animals for surgery, administer anesthesia, organize the surgical instruments, and watch the animals' vital signs.

During routine exams, veterinary technicians restrain animals, clean ears, and clip nails. They take care of pharmaceutical equipment and other supplies and make sure they are in stock. Veterinary technicians take and develop X rays, test for parasites, and examine samples taken from the animal's body, such as blood or stool. About 50 percent of a veterinary technician's duties involve laboratory testing. They make careful notes, write reports, and enter information on computers.

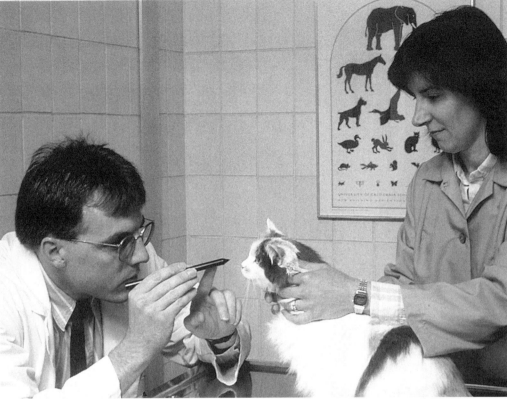

A veterinary technician works closely with a veterinarian to keep a cat still while he examines its eyes.

Veterinary technicians assist the veterinarian with surgical procedures. This generally means preparing the animal for surgery by shaving the incision area and applying an antibacterial medicine to the skin. Surgical anesthesia is administered and controlled by veterinary technicians. Throughout the surgery process, technicians keep track of the surgical instruments and watch the animal's vital signs. If an animal is very ill and has no chance for survival, veterinary technicians may

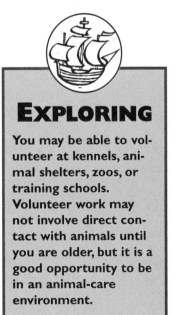

EXPLORING

You may be able to volunteer at kennels, animal shelters, zoos, or training schools. Volunteer work may not involve direct contact with animals until you are older, but it is a good opportunity to be in an animal-care environment.

have to help in putting it to sleep. Veterinary technicians may also assist the veterinarian in trying to determine the cause of an animal's death.

Veterinary technicians must enjoy working with animals. They must be able to handle animals that are sick, frightened, or violent. They must be able to talk to pet owners, to be sympathetic, and clearly explain procedures, treatments, and care instructions. An important skill for a veterinary technician is the ability to follow the veterinarian's instructions.

Most veterinary technicians work in clinical or private settings. Some work in research labs, zoos, rural areas, or in animal training. Jobs in zoos are the most desired and the hardest to get, since there are only a few zoos in each state.

WEB SITES FOR VET TECHS

Good News for Pets
http://www.goodnewsforpets.com/

The Pet Center
http://www.thepetcenter.com/

Veterinary Learning Systems
http://www.vetlearn.com/

Vet Team
http://www.vetteam.com/

NetVet
http://www.avma.org/netvet/vet.htm

Education and Training

It will be important for you to take high school courses in science, computers, chemistry, math, and health. Get any experience with animals that you can.

After high school, you must graduate from a two-year program that is accredited by the American Veterinary Medical

Association. There are also some four-year programs that lead to a bachelor's degree. These programs include courses in chemistry, mathematics, communications, ethics, computers, nutrition, medical terminology, veterinary anatomy, and clinical procedures, such as radiography. You also receive practical training working with live animals.

Earnings

Salaries for veterinary technicians in private practices and clinics range from $15,000 for recent graduates to $40,000 for experienced supervising technicians. There are higher paying jobs in zoos and in research, but there are few openings in these areas.

Outlook

Employment for veterinary technicians will grow about as fast as the average through 2008. There will be a steady demand for qualified technicians as pet ownership continues to grow.

FOR MORE INFO

For information on careers and resources, contact the following organizations:
American Veterinary Medical Association
1931 North Meacham Road, Suite 100
Schaumburg, IL 60173-4360
Tel: 800-248-2862
Web: http://www.avma.org/

For more information on zoo veterinary technology and positions, contact:
Association of Zoo Veterinary Technicians
c/o Louisville Zoo
PO Box 37250
Louisville, KY 40233
Tel: 502-451-0440
Web: http://www.worldzoo.org/azvt/

North American Veterinary Technician Association
PO Box 224
Battle Ground, IN 47920
Web: http://www.avma.org/navta/

RELATED JOBS

Animal Caretakers
Animal Shelter Employees
Veterinarians
Zookeepers
Zoologists

Wildlife Photographers

Photo Galleries on the Web

These Web sites all have photo galleries, as well as lots of information about wildlife, habitat conservation, and endangered species.

U.S. Fish and Wildlife Service
http://www.fws.gov/

National Wildlife Federation
http://www.nwf.org/nwf/

World Wildlife Fund
http://www.world wildlife.org/

Zooweb: How to Take Great Pictures at the Zoo
http://www.zooweb.net/ photos.htm

What Wildlife Photographers Do

Wildlife photographers take photographs and make films of animals in their natural environment. Wildlife photographers provide the photographs for science publications, research reports, textbooks, newspapers, magazines, and many other printed materials. Films are used in research and for professional and public education.

Wildlife photographers often find themselves in swamps, deserts, jungles, at the tops of trees or in underground tunnels, swimming in the ocean or hanging from the side of a mountain. They may shoot pictures of the tiniest insects or the largest mammals.

Some wildlife photographers specialize in one family or species or in one region or area. For example, some wildlife photographers may shoot chimpanzees in their various habitats around the world. Another photographer might shoot various species of birds that live in the southwestern United States.

Like other professional photographers, wildlife photographers must know about light, camera settings, lenses, film, and filters. In addition, they must be able to take pictures without disturbing the animals or natural settings that they photograph. To do this, they must research the animals and plants they use as subjects before they go into the wild.

Wildlife photographers do not necessarily need to be zoologists, although a background in biology or zoology is helpful for this career. After many years of experience, wildlife photographers often become experts in the behavior of the animals they photograph. It is also possible for zoologists who use photography in their research to eventually become expert wildlife photographers.

The technological advances in photographic equipment and the expertise of wildlife photographers have contributed much to scientific knowledge about animal behavior, new species, evolution, and animals' roles in preserving or changing the environment.

EXPLORING

• Take classes in photography, media arts (film, sound recording), and life sciences.

• Join photography clubs or enter contests that encourage you to use camera equipment.

• Learn how to use different types of film, lenses, and filters.

• Practice taking pictures of birds and animals at parks, nature centers, and zoos.

• Watch nature shows and videos to learn more about both animal behavior and filming animals in the wild.

BE A PRO:
TIPS FOR TAKING
WILDLIFE PHOTOS

• Study the animals you want to photograph before you go out. Learn about their eating, sleeping, and other behaviors so you will know what to expect.

• Plan ahead and take the right kind and amount of film you need. Consider the light and weather conditions. Take extra camera batteries.

• Wear dark clothes that blend in with surroundings.

• Don't stand where you will stick out like a sore thumb. Stay in shadows near trees or shrubs.

• Keep your distance.

• Be patient and alert. While you are waiting to take a photo or shoot film of a particular animal, you may see dozens of other opportunities to shoot other birds, insects, and animals around you.

Education and Training

There are no formal education requirements for becoming a wildlife photographer. A high school diploma is recommended for this career, and earning a college degree will help you learn about both photography and biology. A bachelor of arts in photography or film with a minor in biology would prepare you well for a career as a wildlife photographer. During your education, you should try to gain practical experience and build a portfolio of your work.

Wildlife photographers must not risk the well being of any animal to take a picture. They must show concern for the environment in their work. They must use common sense and not anger or frighten any animals while trying to take a picture.

Earnings

Full-time wildlife photographers earn average salaries of about $25,000 to $38,000 a year. Most wildlife photographers work as freelancers. Wildlife photographers who combine scientific training and photographic expertise usually start at higher salaries than other photographers. It can be difficult to earn a living as a wildlife photographer, so you may have to supplement your income with another occupation or do other kinds of photography until you earn a reputation.

Outlook

Employment of photographers will increase more slowly than the average through 2008. The demand for new photographs and videos of animals in their natural habitats should remain strong in research, education, communication, and entertainment.

FOR MORE INFO

For information on photography careers, contact the following organizations.

American Film Institute
2021 North Western Avenue
Los Angeles, CA 90027
Tel: 323-856-7600
Email: info@afionline.org
Web: http://www.afionline.org/

Professional Photographers of America
229 Peachtree Street, NE, No. 2200
Atlanta, GA 30303-2206
Tel: 800-786-6277
Email: membership@ppa.world.org
Web: http://www.ppa.com/

Wildlife Research Photography
PO Box 3628
Mammoth Lakes, CA 93546-3628
Tel: 760-924-8632
Web: http://www.moose395.net/

RELATED JOBS

Biologists
Cinematographers
Film Directors and Producers
Naturalists
Photographers
Zoologists

Zoo and Aquarium Curators

How Do Zoos Get Their Animals?

Zoos buy most of their animals from regular dealers who collect them from all over the world. Sometimes a zoo will send out its own collecting expedition. Animals are also obtained by trading with other zoos. Animals that are hard to collect and transport, or that are difficult to breed in cap- tivity, are the most expensive. Lions are rel- atively inexpensive ani- mals because they are easy to breed and raise in zoos. White rhinocer- oses are among the most expensive.

What Zoo and Aquarium Curators Do

Zoo and aquarium curators are in charge of the care of the animals that live at zoos and aquariums. Curators have expert knowledge of the habitats, daily care, medical plans, diet, and social habits of the animals in their care. They work closely with zookeepers, veterinarians, exhibit designers, and teachers. They develop exhibits, educational programs, and visitor services. They supervise the daily activities of the assistant curators, zookeepers, administrative staff, researchers, students, and volunteers. They oversee important research that shows whether the animals' activities, habitats, and diets are the best they can be. Zoo and aquarium curators also keep inventories of animals, attend scientific and research conferences, prepare bud- gets, and write reports.

Curators work with other institutions, too. For example, they might share research

San Diego Zoo

Zoo curators are responsible for bringing new animals, such as this young leopard, to live in their zoos.

information or arrange to loan an animal to another zoo for breeding. Curators coordinate purchases from animal dealers, and arrange for collection of nonendangered species from the wild.

Large zoos and aquariums often have a general curator to oversee the entire collection of animals, plus a curator for each division. For instance, a large zoo might have a general curator, a bird curator, a reptile curator, and a mammal curator. General curators work closely with the zoo or aquarium director and other members of the staff to make long-term plans and develop policies that will keep the facility running smoothly.

EXPLORING

• Volunteer at zoos or aquariums, animal shelters, wildlife rehabilitation centers, stables, or veterinary hospitals.

• Here are some reading suggestions:
Zoo Animals: A Smithsonian Guide by Michael Robinson and David Challinor (IDG Books Worldwide, 1995).
Amphibians: Creatures of the Land and Water by Edward J. Maruska (Franklin Watts, Inc., 1994).
Zoo Clues: Making the Most of Your Visit to the Zoo by Sheldon Gerstenfeld (Puffin Books, 1993).

Education and Training

High school courses in the sciences, mathematics, computer sciences, language, and speech will help you prepare for a career as a curator.

After high school, you need to earn at least a bachelor's degree in one of the biological sciences, such as zoology, ecology, biology, mammalogy, or ornithology. A master's or doctoral degree is often required to work in large institutions.

In addition to advanced academic training, it takes years of on-the-job experience to learn about animal husbandry. Many curators start out by volunteering as zookeepers and work their way up over the years, getting experience at the same time as earning their degrees.

Curators who work for zoos and aquariums must love animals, but they must also get along well with people. Management skills and leadership ability are important. Curators must also have writing ability and research experience.

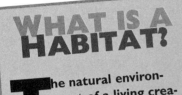

WHAT IS A HABITAT?

The natural environment of a living creature is called its *habitat*. The term is applied to the three large life zones:

1. **Salt Water** (which is further divided into depth zones)

2. **Fresh Water** (running water and standing water)

3. **Land** (divided into climatic or vegetation zones)

Even when a habitat is ideal for a certain species, the species may not live there because of geographic and climatic barriers or biological barriers. *Geographic and climatic barriers* include water (for land animals), land (for water animals), high mountains, and temperature extremes. *Biological barriers* include the absence of food or the presence of enemies.

Earnings

Salaries for zoo and aquarium curators depend on the size and location of the facility, whether it is privately or publicly owned, the size of its budget, and the curator's responsibilities, educational background, and experience. Yearly salaries for curators can range from a low of $20,000 to a high of $79,000. General curators in large cities earn average salaries of around $40,000.

Outlook

There are fewer than 200 professionally operated zoos, aquariums, wildlife parks, and oceanariums in North America. Growth of new zoos is slow, and the current number of jobs at zoos, aquariums, wildlife parks, and oceanariums is far smaller than the number of people who apply for them. There may be more opportunities at private conservation centers than at public zoos and aquariums.

FOR MORE INFO

For further information, contact one of the following organizations:

American Zoo and Aquarium Association
8403 Colesville Road, Suite 710
Silver Spring, MD 20910-3314
Web: http://www.aza.org/

American Association of Zoo Keepers, Inc.
3601 S.W. 29th Street, Suite 133
Topeka, KS 66614
Web: http://aazk.org/

For information on training, contact the following educational institutions:

Friends University of Wichita
2100 West University
Wichita, KS 67213
Tel: 800-794-6945
Web: http://www.friends.edu/science/zoo.htm

Santa Fe Community College Zoo Studies Programs
3000 Northwest 83rd Street
Gainesville, FL 32606
Tel: 352-395-5000
Web: http://www.santafe.cc.fl.us/

Zoo and Aquarium Directors

What Zoo and Aquarium Directors Do

Zoo and aquarium directors' jobs are like those of company presidents or school principals. They are responsible mainly for the important business affairs of their institutions. Directors are in charge of all the institution's operations. They develop long-range plans, start new programs, and oversee the animal collection and facilities. Directors of public zoos and aquariums usually report to a governing board, a group of people who set policies and make rules for the institution, such as how money is spent. Directors make sure those policies and rules are followed.

Directors plan budgets based on fund-raising programs, government grants, and private donations. They meet with curators to discuss animal acquisitions, educational programs, research projects, and other activities. Directors of larger zoos and aquariums may give speeches, appear at fund-raising events, and repre-

A zoo director follows up on the health and well-being of a recent acquisition.

sent their organizations on television or radio. A major part of the director's job is seeing that the zoo or aquarium has enough financial resources. Directors also spend a great deal of time working with architects, engineers, contractors, and artisans on renovation and construction of facilities, exhibits, and other projects.

Directors are responsible for informing the public about what is going on at the zoo or aquarium. They hold interviews

EXPLORING

• Volunteer at animal shelters, zoos, kennels, pet stores, stables, veterinary facilities, or anywhere you can get experience working directly with animals.
• Visit your local zoos and aquariums often. Attend events and educational programs they offer.

with reporters, write annual reports, and write articles for newsletters, newspapers, and magazines. Directors also may work on committees for conservation organizations or with universities and scientists to support conservation research.

Education and Training

To become a zoo or aquarium director, you need a well-rounded education. You need at least a bachelor's degree in business management or administration. Most directors have master's degrees and many in larger institutions hold doctoral degrees. A background in both science and business will make you a desirable candidate for employment.

Classes in zoology, biology, accounting, economics, and general business are important. Courses in sociology, speech,

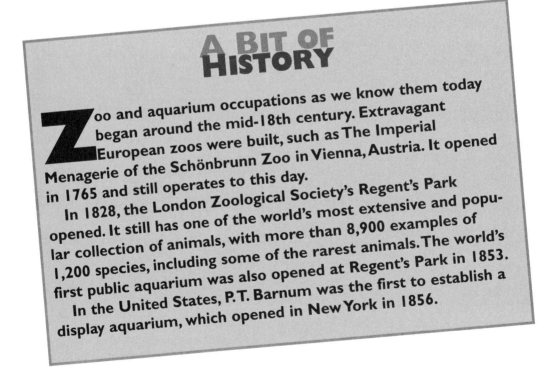

A BIT OF HISTORY

Zoo and aquarium occupations as we know them today began around the mid-18th century. Extravagant European zoos were built, such as The Imperial Menagerie of the Schönbrunn Zoo in Vienna, Austria. It opened in 1765 and still operates to this day.

In 1828, the London Zoological Society's Regent's Park opened. It still has one of the world's most extensive and popular collection of animals, with more than 8,900 examples of 1,200 species, including some of the rarest animals. The world's first public aquarium was also opened at Regent's Park in 1853.

In the United States, P.T. Barnum was the first to establish a display aquarium, which opened in New York in 1856.

and debate will improve your ability to speak to the public and to reporters, as well as communicate with governing boards and staff members.

Earnings

Zoo and aquarium directors earn anywhere from $28,000 to $80,000 a year. A few directors in large metropolitan areas earn $100,000 or more. These salaries aren't very high, considering their responsibilities. Some directors earn extra income from writing books and public speaking engagements.

Outlook

There will be few openings for zoo and aquarium directors in the next ten years. There are fewer than 200 professionally operated zoos, aquariums, wildlife parks, and oceanariums in North America. Each of them employs only one director. Competition for these jobs will be extremely strong.

Because of the slow growth in the number of new zoos, job

FOR MORE INFO

For more information, contact:
American Zoo and Aquarium Association
8403 Colesville Road, Suite 710
Silver Spring, MD 20910-3314
Tel: 301-562-0777
Web: http://www.aza.org/

American Association of Zoo Keepers, Inc.
3601 S.W. 29th Street, Suite 133
Topeka, KS 66614
Web: http://aazk.org/

openings are not expected to grow. The outlook for aquariums is somewhat brighter due to the planned construction of several new facilities.

RELATED JOBS

Animal Caretakers
Animal Handlers
Animal Shelter Employees
Veterinarians
Veterinary Technicians
Zoo and Aquarium Curators
Zookeepers
Zoologists

Zookeepers

What Zookeepers Do

Zookeepers are the daily caretakers for zoo animals. They prepare the animals' diets, clean and maintain cages, and watch animals' behavior. They give vitamins or medications to the animals, fill water containers in their cages, and safely move animals from one location to another. Zookeepers provide enrichment devices for the animals, such as ropes for monkeys to swing on. They regulate environmental factors, such as temperature and humidity, and bathe and groom animals.

Zookeepers work closely with other zoo staff on research, conservation, and animal reproduction. They also talk to zoo visitors, giving information and answering questions about the animals they care for. Sometimes zookeepers have to discourage visitors from teasing or feeding the animals.

Zookeepers have many custodial and maintenance tasks, which can be physically demanding and dirty. They must deal with live food items and body wastes. They must work both indoors and outdoors, in all kinds of weather. Zookeepers sometimes face the risk of injury and disease.

Keepers often work with one particular group of animals such as primates or birds, but in some zoos (usually smaller ones) keepers may care for a wide range of species. Zookeepers become experts on the species and the individual animals in their care. They observe and understand eating, sleeping, mating, and social habits. They notice even small changes in animals' appearance and behavior so that any illness or injury can be taken care of right away.

Education and Training

For entry-level zookeeping positions you need a college degree. Degrees in animal science, zoology, marine biology, conservation biology, wildlife management, or animal behavior are the best choices. A few colleges and junior colleges offer a specialized curriculum for zookeepers. Animal care experience, such as zoo volunteer work or veterinary hospital work, is important.

EXPLORING

• Most zoos and aquariums have Web sites with information about the institution and its programs and career opportunities. For links to zoos around the world and other zoo information, explore this site:
ZooWeb
http://www.zooweb.net/

• Many zoos and aquariums offer classes about animals and conservation. They also offer volunteer opportunities, such as Explorers or Junior Zookeeper programs. Volunteer duties may include cleaning enclosures, preparing food, or handling domesticated animals.

• You may also find volunteer opportunities at animal shelters, boarding kennels, wildlife rehabilitation centers, stables, or animal hospitals.

NOTABLE U.S. ZOOS

Chicago Zoological Park (Brookfield Zoo), Brookfield, Illinois, has one of the largest and most varied animal collections in the United States.

Cincinnati Zoo, Cincinnati, Ohio, is one of the oldest and largest zoos in the United States. It was among the first to exhibit animals in cageless areas that reproduced natural habitats and was the first U.S. zoo to devote a major building to insects.

Detroit Zoological Park, Royal Oak, Michigan, has cageless exhibits that are grouped by continents.

International Wildlife Conservation Park (Bronx Zoo), Bronx, New York, has a collection of very rare animals. It opened in 1899.

Lincoln Park Zoological Garden (Lincoln Park Zoo), Chicago, Illinois, was founded in 1868. It is the oldest zoo in the United States and has a collection of about 2,000 animals.

Milwaukee County Zoological Park, Milwaukee, Wisconsin, has natural settings for almost all the animals. It has several underwater viewing areas.

National Zoological Park, Washington, DC, has more than 4,000 animals.

Philadelphia Zoological Garden (Philadelphia Zoo), Philadelphia, Pennsylvania, was founded in 1859 and opened exhibits in 1874. The zoo was a pioneer in animal health research.

St. Louis Zoological Park, St. Louis, Missouri, has a large collection of animals and natural-habitat settings.

San Diego Zoo, San Diego, California, exhibits most of its animals outdoors in tropical and subtropical settings. It has a reproduction program for endangered species.

Some major zoos offer formal zookeeper training courses, as well as on-the-job training programs. These programs are available to students who are studying areas related to animal science and care. Participation in these programs can lead to full-time positions as zookeepers.

Earnings

The zookeeper's salary can range from just above minimum wage ($5.15 an hour) to more than $40,000 a year, depending on the keeper's education and experience and the zoo's location and finances. The highest salaries are usually in larger cities.

Outlook

There are only about 200 professionally operated zoos, aquariums, and wildlife parks in North America. Approximately 350 new zookeeper jobs become available each year. Zoos are becoming more involved in animal preservation.

FOR MORE INFO

For further information, contact:
American Association of Zoo Keepers, Inc.
3601 S.W. 29th, Suite 133
Topeka, KS 66614
Web: http://aazk.ind.net/

American Zoo and Aquarium Association
8403 Colesville Road, Suite 710
Silver Spring, MD 20910-3314
Web: http://www.aza.org/

There will be a growing need for zookeepers to work in preservation of endangered species and in educating the public about conservation.

RELATED JOBS

Animal Caretakers
Animal Handlers
Animal Shelter Employees
Veterinarians
Veterinary Technicians
Zoo and Aquarium Curators
Zoo and Aquarium Directors
Zoologists

Zoologists

What Zoologists Do

Zoologists are biologists who study animals. They usually specialize in one animal group. *Entomologists* are experts on insects. *Ornithologists* study birds. *Mammalogists* focus on mammals. *Herpetologists* specialize in reptiles. *Ichthyologists* study fish. Some zoologists specialize even more and focus on a specific part or aspect of an animal. For example, a zoologist might study single-celled organisms, a particular variety of fish, or the behavior of one group of animals, such as elephants or bees.

Some zoologists are primarily teachers. Others spend most of their time doing research. Nearly all zoologists spend a major portion of their time at the computer. Most zoologists spend very little time outdoors (an average of two to eight weeks per year). In fact, junior scientists often spend more time in the field than senior scientists do. Senior scientists coordinate research, supervise other

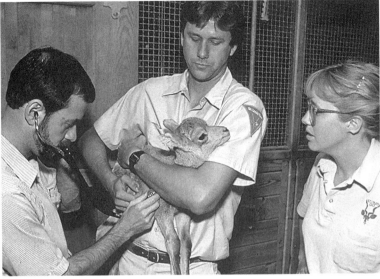

A mammalogist at a nature preserve does a routine check on one of the preserve's animals as part of an ongoing research study.

workers, and try to find funding. Raising money is an extremely important activity for zoologists who do work for government agencies or universities.

Basic research zoologists conduct experiments on live or dead animals, in a laboratory or in natural surroundings. They make discoveries that might help humans. Such research in the past has led to discoveries about nutrition, aging, food production, and pest control. Some research zoologists work in the field with wild animals, such as whales. They trace their movements with radio transmitters and observe their eating habits, mating patterns, and other behavior. Researchers use all kinds of laboratory chemicals and equipment such as dissecting tools,

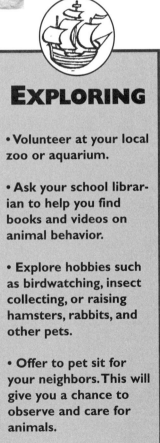

EXPLORING

• Volunteer at your local zoo or aquarium.

• Ask your school librarian to help you find books and videos on animal behavior.

• Explore hobbies such as birdwatching, insect collecting, or raising hamsters, rabbits, and other pets.

• Offer to pet sit for your neighbors. This will give you a chance to observe and care for animals.

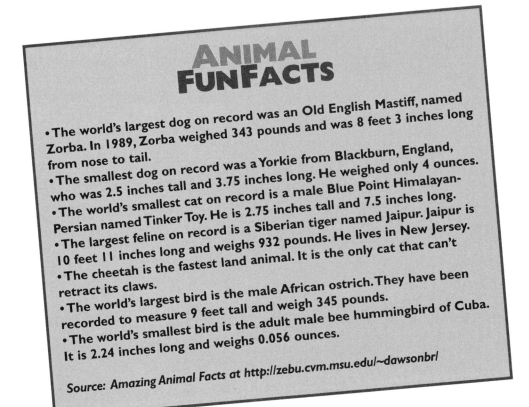

ANIMAL FUNFACTS

- The world's largest dog on record was an Old English Mastiff, named Zorba. In 1989, Zorba weighed 343 pounds and was 8 feet 3 inches long from nose to tail.
- The smallest dog on record was a Yorkie from Blackburn, England, who was 2.5 inches tall and 3.75 inches long. He weighed only 4 ounces.
- The world's smallest cat on record is a male Blue Point Himalayan-Persian named Tinker Toy. He is 2.75 inches tall and 7.5 inches long.
- The largest feline on record is a Siberian tiger named Jaipur. Jaipur is 10 feet 11 inches long and weighs 932 pounds. He lives in New Jersey.
- The cheetah is the fastest land animal. It is the only cat that can't retract its claws.
- The world's largest bird is the male African ostrich. They have been recorded to measure 9 feet tall and weigh 345 pounds.
- The world's smallest bird is the adult male bee hummingbird of Cuba. It is 2.24 inches long and weighs 0.056 ounces.

Source: Amazing Animal Facts at http://zebu.cvm.msu.edu/~dawsonbr/

microscopes, slides, electron microscopes, and other sophisticated machinery.

Zoologists in applied research use basic research to solve problems in medicine, conservation, and aquarium and zoo work. For example, applied researchers may develop a new drug for people or animals, a new pesticide, or a new type of pet food.

Many zoologists teach in colleges and universities while they do their own research. Some zoologists manage zoos and aquariums. Still others work for government agencies, private businesses, and research organizations.

Education and Training

Science classes, especially in biology, are important if you want to become a zoologist. You should also study English, communications, and computer science.

After high school, you must go to college to earn a bachelor's degree. A master's or doctoral degree is usually also required. You do not need to specialize until you enter a master's degree program.

Earnings

Beginning salaries in private industry average $29,000 a year for zoologists with bachelor's degrees in biological science. Those with master's degrees earn $34,000 a year. Zoologists with doctoral degrees earn about $46,000 a year. General biological scientists who work for the federal government earn average salaries of about $48,600.

FOR MORE INFO

For information about all areas of zoology, contact:
Society for Integrative and Comparative Biology
1313 Dolley Madison Boulevard, Suite 402
McLean, VA 22201
Tel: 800-955-1236
Web: http://www.sicb.org

For information about zoological activities and organizations, schools, internships, and job opportunities, contact:
American Institute of Biological Sciences
1444 Eye Street, NW, Suite 200
Washington, DC 20005
Tel: 202-628-1500
Web: http://www.aibs.org

Outlook

Although job growth in the field of zoology has been slow in recent years, that should change in the early 21st century. This is because there is more interest in preserving the environment. There will be a lot of competition for research jobs.

Glossary

accredited: Approved as meeting established standards for providing good training and education. This approval is usually given by an independent organization of professionals to a school or a program in a school. Compare **certified** and **licensed**.

apprentice: A person who is learning a trade by working under the supervision of a skilled worker. Apprentices often receive classroom instruction in addition to their supervised practical experience.

apprenticeship: 1. A program for training apprentices (see apprentice). 2. The period of time when a person is an apprentice. In highly skilled trades, apprenticeships may last three or four years.

associate's degree: An academic rank or title granted by a community or junior college or similar institution to graduates of a two-year program of education beyond high school.

bachelor's degree: An academic rank or title given to a person who has completed a four-year program of study at a college or university. Also called an undergraduate degree or baccalaureate.

certified: Approved as meeting established requirements for skill, knowledge, and experience in a particular field. People are certified by the organization of professionals in their field. Compare **accredited** and **licensed**.

community college: A public two-year college, attended by students who do not live at the college. Graduates of a community college receive an associate degree and may transfer to a four-year college or university to complete a bachelor's degree. Compare **junior college** and **technical college**.

diploma: A certificate or document given by a school to show that a person has completed a course or has graduated from the school.

doctorate: An academic rank or title (the highest) granted by a graduate school to a person who has completed a two- to three-year program after having received a master's degree.

fringe benefit: A payment or benefit to an employee in addition to regular wages or salary. Examples of fringe benefits include a pension, a paid vacation, and health or life insurance.

graduate school: A school that people may attend after they have received their bachelor's degree. People who complete an educational program at a graduate school earn a master's degree or a doctorate.

intern: An advanced student (usually one with at least some college training) in a professional field who is employed in a job that is intended to provide supervised practical experience for the student.

internship: 1. The position or job of an intern (see intern). 2. The period of time when a person is an intern.

junior college: A two-year college that offers courses like those in the first half of a four-year college program. Graduates of a junior college usually receive an associate degree and may transfer to a four-year college or university to complete a bachelor's degree. Compare **community college.**

liberal arts: The subjects covered by college courses that develop broad general knowledge rather than specific occupational skills. The liberal arts are often considered to include philosophy, literature and the arts, history, language, and some courses in the social sciences and natural sciences.

licensed: Having formal permission from the proper authority to carry out an activity that would be illegal without that permission. For example, a person may be licensed to practice medicine or to drive a car. Compare **certified**.

major: (in college) The academic field in which a student specializes and receives a degree.

master's degree: An academic rank or title granted by a graduate school to a person who has completed a one- or two-year program after having received a bachelor's degree.

pension: An amount of money paid regularly by an employer to a former employee after he or she retires from working.

private: 1. Not owned or controlled by the government (such as private industry or a private employment agency). 2. Intended only for a particular person or group; not open to all (such as a private road or a private club).

public: 1. Provided or operated by the government (such as a public library). 2. Open and available to everyone (such as a public meeting).

regulatory: Having to do with the rules and laws for carrying out an activity. A regulatory agency, for example, is a government organization that sets up required procedures for how certain things should be done.

scholarship: A gift of money to a student to help the student pay for further education.

social studies: Courses of study (such as civics, geography, and history) that deal with how human societies work.

starting salary: Salary paid to a newly hired employee. The starting salary is usually a smaller amount than is paid to a more experienced worker.

technical college: A private or public college offering two- or four-year programs in technical subjects. Technical colleges offer courses in both general and technical subjects and award associate degrees and bachelor's degrees.

technician: A worker with specialized practical training in a mechanical or scientific subject who works under the supervision of scientists, engineers, or other professionals. Technicians typically receive two years of college-level education after high school.

technologist: A worker in a mechanical or scientific field with more training than a technician. Technologists typically must have between two and four years of college-level education after high school.

undergraduate: A student at a college or university who has not yet received a degree.

undergraduate degree: See **bachelor's degree**.

union: An organization whose members are workers in a particular industry or company. The union works to gain better wages, benefits, and working conditions for its members. Also called a labor union or trade union.

vocational school: A public or private school that offers training in one or more skills or trades. Compare **technical college**.

wage: Money that is paid in return for work done, especially money paid on the basis of the number of hours or days worked.

Index of Job Titles

adoption counselors, 14, 17

animal breeders and
    technicians, 6-9

animal caretakers, 10-13

animal control workers, 15

animal shelter workers, 14-17

animal trainers, 18-21

aquarists, 22-25

aquatic biologists, 26

artificial insemination
    technicians, 6

artificial-breeding technicians, 6

basic research zoologists, 83

beekeepers, 32

biological scientists, 26

biologists, 26-29, 82

botanists, 26

breeders, 6-9, 37

cattle breeders, 6

conservationists, 43

curators, 70, 71

dairy farmers, 31

dog groomers, 50-53

dog trainers, 20

dog walkers, 54

ecologists, 42

entomologists, 82

environmental educators, 42

farmers, 30-33

farriers, 35

fish and wildlife wardens, 43

herpetologists, 82

horse and dog breeders, 6

horse grooms, 34-37

horse trainers, 20, 21

hotwalkers, 35

humane educators, 15

humane investigators, 15

ichthyologists, 82

junior scientists, 82

kennel attendants, 14

kennel workers, 17

life scientists, 26

livestock farmers, 31

mammalogists, 82

marine biologists, 38-41

microbiologists, 28

naturalists, 42-45

nature resource managers, 42

ornithologists, 82

park rangers, 46-49

pet groomers, 50-53

pet sitters, 54-57
pet sitting technicians, 56
poultry farmers, 31

range managers, 43

senior scientists, 82
sheep ranchers, 31
shelter administrators, 16, 17
shelter managers, 15, 16

trainers, 18-21, 34

veterinarians, 58-61, 70

veterinary assistants, 10
veterinary technicians, 62-65

wildlife conservationists, 42
wildlife managers, 43
wildlife photographers, 66-69
wildlife shelter workers, 10

zoo and aquarium curators,
    70-73
zoo and aquarium directors,
    74-77
zookeepers, 22, 70, 78-81
zoologists, 26, 67, 82-85

Animals on the Web

All for Kids! Animals
http://www.cache.net/kids/animals.html

Kids World 2000—Animals, Zoos & Aquariums
http://www.now2000.com/kids/zoos.shtml

National Audubon Society
http://www.audubon.org/

National Wildlife Federation
http://www.nwf.org/

Nearctica
http://www.nearctica.com/family/kids/kanimals.htm

Sea World/Busch Gardens Animal Information
http://www.seaworld.org/

Sierra Club
http://www.sierraclub.org/

U.S. Fish & Wildlife Service
http://www.fws.gov/

Wildlife Web
http://www.selu.com/bio/wildlife/index.html

World Wildlife Fund
http://worldwildlife.org/